THE BOY FROM ROD ALLEY

THE BOY FROM ROD ALLEY

Moments of lost times made new
Elusive, fragmentary, true

John Loveday

Matador
9 Priory Business Park,
Wistow Road, Kibworth Beauchamp,
Leicestershire. LE8 0RX
Tel: 0116 279 2299
Email: books@troubador.co.uk
Web: www.troubador.co.uk/matador
Twitter: @matadorbooks

ISBN 978 1789017 564

British Library Cataloguing in Publication Data.
A catalogue record for this book is available from the British Library.

Printed and bound in Great Britain by 4edge Limited
Typeset in 11pt Sabon MT by Troubador Publishing Ltd, Leicester, UK

Matador is an imprint of Troubador Publishing Ltd

Cover: oil-painting, Rod Alley, by the author.
Cover design and author portrait, Julian Loveday

To the memory of Hans Lindenmayer, former prisoner-of-war, who chose to stay in England, and loved learning of earlier times in his adopted village. Also to my cousin Russell Bower, with whom I have shared many experiences throughout life, and who suggested, long ago, that I should write about childhood.

I try to write a hope for those
Once true-life characters who live
Inside my book. May my words give
Us chance to linger when the pages close.

AUTHOR'S NOTE

The characters in the book are called by their true names. In respect of anyone not seen as favourably as most, I should say that I have not recorded anything other than the manner in which people represented themselves to my boyhood eyes. It has been my intention, throughout, to avoid hindsight from an adult point of view.

This account of childhood reflects the way memory works, by making changes of scene or subject abruptly, often without linking words.

The name Rod Alley used to puzzle me. Eventually, I noticed that an alley could be a way between lines of trees, or shrubs, and found that 'rod' was an old name for osiers. I had painted them from a window in Rod Alley in 1949 (see cover).

CONTENTS

CHAPTER 1

From our door, the gravel path was level as far as the May tree. From there, it sloped to an iron gate and railings. Beyond the railings, the little road, of stones and mud or stones and dust, crossed in front of the pond. Nobody who lived here called it the pond. It was a pit, Rod Alley pit, and the row of houses made Rod Alley Row. The pit was long, the length of about six of the ten houses and the spaces between them. It had steep sides, but was shallow at the ends, where the cattle came to stand in the water to drink. Usually they lifted their tails to piss at the same time. They stayed a while, then went back to graze on the Green. The water lay undisturbed except by wind or ducks. Away from those ends, it was deep, and in the middle somewhere it went down, down, down so deep that you did not dare to think of it. You quickly talked of something else, and the surface reflected the sky, just still or broken by ripples.

Sometimes, 'down, down, down' made you think of Australia.

Beyond the pit was the 'Council Road'. Buses from Norwich turned round here at the wide space where Abbey Road met the main road. Abbey Road sloped away between stretches of the Green, towards the corner called Chattergate. The place probably had its name because the women who lived there long ago called to each other across the little yard from their houses on three sides, but nobody knew. My friend Alfred Etteridge lived there. His mother always called him Eric. I didn't know why and never asked him.

The road we lived in was no longer to be called by its old name. It was now Post Office Terrace. My father was angry. He said we lived in Rod Alley Row, and Post Office Terrace was to be written on our letters because that sounded posher in the opinion of Mrs Moore, who ran the Post Office, which was the tiny shop at the Green end of the road. Dad said he would still write Rod Alley Row because that was where we lived, and the name couldn't be changed just because Mrs Moore wanted it changed.

Jack Kemp the postman, in his dark blue uniform decorated by bits of red, with his rosy face, and his big brown bag, brought letters that sometimes had the new name on them. It seemed odd, but strangely posher.

The house called Sunnyside could be seen from Rod Alley Row if you looked towards Chattergate. It was off to the left, the north edge of the Green, facing south. From his desk in one of the two big bay windows, Grandad could see almost the whole of the Green. In the farthest corner, away to the right, anyone walking would appear very small indeed.

Grandad must have been proud to own Sunnyside. When he was a young man, he lived in Rod Alley Row. He had set his mind on one day being able to buy Sunnyside for his growing family. His dream came true, and he was able to take his Edith and the younger children of their family of ten to live there, to look across to the old home in Rod Alley. When his son Tom married, he was given the house where he had grown up. I always knew how old my dad was, because he was born in 1900. Perhaps the May tree was planted in Grandad's day. Dad called it 'the bloody old May tree', and decided to cut it down to let more light into the living-room front window, which was also shadowed by being further back than the main front part of the house.

It was a beautiful tree in spring, full of red blossom.

My grandfather sat at his desk, in his grey suit which he always wore, with his longish silvery hair, which had been ginger, and worked at the books in which he kept the records of his business. From these heavy ledgers he took the details for bills, which were written with great care to look as neat as any human hand could make them. If he made the smallest error, it was removed by scraping with a specially sharpened knife. Grandad took pride in his skill with that knife. He took pride in his whole business. He said that his threshing machines could do a better job than any others. Except for the steam engines, everything was built by his father, his uncle, and their workmen.

People said that he looked like Mr Lloyd George. I didn't know who Mr Lloyd George was, or what he looked like, except that he must have looked something like my grandfather. When I learned he'd been Prime Minister in the Great War and after it, he seemed to be worth looking like. But Grandad was not pleased when he was greeted as 'Mr Lloyd George' in a Norwich street.

When I was only two years old, Mum said, he had bought me a model steam engine. Sometime later, I was able to see it work, and later still I played with it. A small methylated spirit burner, with a flame lighted by a match, heated the water in the boiler, and soon a piston was working to make the flywheel spin, as on a real steam traction engine like those in Grandad's business. It was fixed to a base of tin, so didn't travel forward, but was like the engine in a threshing field. Perhaps he bought it because he thought that I would be an engine man. Mum told me that when I was two I stood for a while in the coal box of a working engine, behind Dad at the steering wheel. I had no memory of that.

The Post Office was built on to the first house in Rod Alley Row. Before Mrs Moore took over, it was run by her parents, 'the old Allingtons' who now lived in the house next-door with their daughter Cecily. Bob Moore was only at home at weekends, going off on Mondays to work as an engineer in Norwich. Mr Moore always seemed cheery when he stepped off the bus on Fridays. I was invited by Mrs Moore to climb the stairs to see her first baby, Peter, a few hours old. Before long, there was a baby girl. There was sadness and a hushing of voices when Bob Moore became ill and soon died. Mrs Moore stayed on, surrounded on three sides by her sweet jars and an assortment of things for sale. When someone was telling her something, she always gave true attention whether the subject was important or not. At the end, she said 'Just fancy!'

In the next two houses were Loveday brothers' families, Uncle Leslie with Ruth and four girls, and my father, Tom, with my mother, Kath, me and my sisters, Thora and Barbara. Beyond us, came the Sturmans, then Uncle Dick and Aunt Dolly, the Whitehands. Next were the Fosters, with daughter Brenda, the Barnards, who were old and always in their 'Sunday best' clothes, the Williamsons, with Iris, and the Watts, with Mary and Oona.

Mr Watts was talking angrily to Mum, at our front door. I knew what it was about. Mum called me out. I went slowly through the passage. She was just outside. Mr Watts had Mary with him.

'Mr Watts says you've been unkind to Mary.'

I didn't answer.

'I've told him it will never happen again. You promise that, John?'

'No.' I said it very quietly.

'It had better not,' said Mr Watts.

'It had better not, indeed,' said Mum. Mary was looking all satisfied. 'Promise,' Mum said. 'You will not do it again.'

'I might.' My voice would only just come.

Mr Watts looked very angry. He said something to Mum. He turned to Mary and they went, and we went in.

'Oh, I felt so embarrassed, standing there,'

Mum said. 'You just keep away from her. You hear me?'

Boys said that Mrs Watts was so fat she couldn't get out of the garden gate. We didn't know if that was true, but it was what we said.

Beyond Rod Alley Row, was the White Horse, a grey-brick pub. It was run by 'the old Petleys', grandparents of my best friend Neville, who lived nearby. People said that Neville went round to find beer left in the bottoms of glasses. Mum said this should not be allowed, a child might catch an illness. But she was also amused. Neville must have got his reddish cheeks and his round head from the old Petleys. We took to each other from the earliest times, my mother said: boys together, when all around were girls.

CHAPTER 2

My mother's brown ducks waddled out of the foundry yard and formed an evenly spaced line that went down the road past the blacksmith's shop towards Rod Alley. From the slope where the cows came down, they launched themselves with happy talk to speed about the water.

By the end of the pit near to the Green, on the verge of grass just before the little road, there was an ancient tree trunk, still standing but long dead. It was hollow. The thick bark showed it had been a willow, perhaps a willow trunk as stout as any willow ever had, every branch gone, perhaps taken off for safety of people who stood beneath them when Grandad was a boy, or earlier still. We went through the opening on one side into the hollow and crumbled a little more of the wood with our fingers. Only a little.

On the living room ceiling, near the staircase door, there was a bulge in the white plaster, shaped like a bum. I must have been told, or had told myself, that it was caused when someone sat too heavily on the bedroom floor. In spite of the stupidity of the story, I half-believed it, as if wanting it to be true.

Similarly, I believed, or half believed, that thunder was the sound of an old woman 'up there' moving furniture about.

When Mum's favourite brother, Uncle Percy, and Aunt Stella came to stay for a few days, Uncle Percy liked me to come to the bedside in the mornings so he could tell me his stories of great sportsmen.

'Get in, and I'll tell you a story about Jack Johnson.'

I got to know some of the people in his stories. I knew Jack Johnson. Sometimes, knowing the stories made them even better. One was about the time the great black boxing champion touched gloves with his opponent (a boxer's token of respect and sportsmanship, Uncle Percy explained, the way of starting the last round. On this occasion, Jack seemed to be thinking that the last round had come when there was another one to go.

'No, Jack, it ain't the last round,' said the opponent.

'It shoo is,' said Jack.

When Uncle Percy told that, he gave his little laugh, and I laughed too.

Aunt Violet lived with Grandad and Grandma, and always liked me coming to Sunnyside. She showed me the coloured board for a game. It had come from Gibbs' Dentifrice. I could read what it said at the edge. It had a tall, ugly man with a great hooked nose and deep lines from his cheeks to his mouth. Aunt Violet said his name was Giant Decay. He was there to stop us from winning, like the snakes in Snakes and Ladders.

'That's Uncle Leslie!'

'That,' she said, 'is not Uncle Leslie.' She was angry. Uncle Leslie was her brother. She had never been angry with me before.

She put the board away, and Giant Decay stayed hidden.

Aunt Violet turned and turned her hands, each one inside the other, out and round and round again, and rubbed the white cream in, and took each finger, one by one, and smoothed and smoothed, and it was done. She smiled, and looked at her nice hands. The smell of Snowfire, it was good to breathe, and kind of posh. The backs of her hands had freckles, light, the pale gold colour of her hair.

Outside the foundry yard, stood all the engines, with their great iron wheels and high funnels, the threshing drums and straw-pitchers of yellow and red, and other machines, making the Green different from anywhere in the world. To look out past the steam engines and other threshing machinery, on to the big Green, was to look out from my grandfather's and father's place of work, their workshops and foundry, and the foundry yard. On the lefthand side, towards Rod Alley, was the blacksmith's shop, which visitors from 'away' called 'the smithy'. On the right, was the grocery and general shop owned by my grandfather's brother Harry, behind which was his main workplace, the bakery, called the 'bake office'.

Dad stopped as we were going toward the way out of the yard and stood near the woodshed to pee in the grass. I didn't need one, so I just stood watching him. His hand was in the way so I couldn't see. There are moments you don't forget, and you don't know why. Bob Turner was an engine man. Either he got riled easily or he pretended it to make amusement for himself. One day, he grumbled words like 'Go away', when we were just inside the foundry yard. When he saw I wouldn't go, he threw a lump of coal at me. I went. But what I never knew was if he meant that I should go, or he liked to make himself look fierce, and the coal was never meant to hit me anyway. He didn't work for Grandad long. He was gone, and never spoken of. He was quite old.

The 'little room' was one we used only in winter. It was between the 'living room', which was the one in which we spent most of the time year-round, and the 'front room', which was for special occasions such as Sundays or Christmas. The 'little room' was warmed by an open fire and the closeness of our bodies. Wooden cupboards on either side of the fireplace held books, games, and comics, ready to tumble out.

There were booklets that made you take an interest in fairies whether you really wanted to or not. To enter the world of fairies, you had to have a pencil, and slowly, inch by inch, scribble evenly over the whole surface. As you did so, small faces and winged bodies appeared, and a story held you, believing. These pages became less interesting as the weeks of that winter went by, because after a while I didn't believe in fairies, and felt free of them forever. Next began the time of adventure in the pages of comics. 'Comics' was the wrong word, because most of the contents were not comic in any way. One story often on my mind was about someone pursuing someone wearing snowshoes that looked like tennis rackets, and the pursued one deceiving the other by strapping on the snowshoes back to front, leaving a clear, false trail that wound across the white page's snow.

A lilac bush grew in the fence between our back garden and Uncle Leslie's. It was just outside the two old privies, which were joined together, side by side. In summertime, the leaves and violet-coloured blossoms almost hid the privies, when you looked towards them, up the path. It was good to have the lovely scent of the lilac blossom as you went to open the door, because in hot weather the other smell was very strong. It would have been a stink without the lilac tree. I thought someone had planted it long ago with that idea. Sometimes, I kept the door open when I sat in there. Nobody could see.

Beyond our back gate into the orchard and the foundry yard, there was a rubbish heap, not big but spread about, a place for old tin cans and other things. Among this was a wasps' nest. On a day when two relatives from the Whitehand side of the family were visiting, called 'Old Uncle John' and Aunt Florrie, I went out after a while to be alone. Something made me want to walk over the heap, and as I didn't know the wasps' nest was there, I stood on it. Wasps buzzed up in a swarm, going in all directions, with some coming at me, on my head, my hands, my legs. As they stung, I called out in pain and terror, scrambling away towards the gate. Already Old Uncle John was coming up the path, with his wife and Mum behind. He

13

knocked wasps off me frantically, and in a few moments they had mostly gone, but one was in his beard, and at first he couldn't get it away. I was crying out still, and Mum was looking after the old lady, who had been stung on her bottom lip. Old Uncle John's wasp was gone. Whether it had escaped or been squashed, I didn't know. I could only think of myself.

When we were back in the house, they were all talking at the same time, asking or telling the best thing to do to ease my pain. The wasps had gone under my shirt and up my short trousers. Someone said, 'Put him in a bath with a blue bag in it.' It was the kind of bag put in the rinsing water after bed sheets and other white things came out of the copper, to make them very white. It was supposed to help with soothing wasp stings.

So, somehow, there had to be water made hot enough for a bath. It took a long time to heat water in summer, but I think Mum already had sticks for a fire under the copper in the scullery, and it was soon heating enough water for a bath. When she brought the 'tin' bath that hung on the outside wall of the shed, everyone told me the pain would soon be gone.

Somewhere around this time, Aunt Maud arrived on the bus. I suppose it was so she could see the old people, who, of course, were her aunt and uncle too. She was Mum's younger sister.

I can't remember how long the water took to heat, nor what was said, except the story of what had just happened, but after a while Old Uncle John and Aunt Florrie had gone. How they had travelled, I don't know. Someone came to fetch them, or they caught a bus to Diss, if it was a Friday, which was the only day it ran. But soon they were gone, and there was only Aunt Maud as the extra person to stand watching as I had to be naked and have my wasp stings pointed out again and be looked at carefully as I got into the blue water. What I was most concerned about was that Aunt Maud was able to look at the bit between my legs. Some people called it a willy, some just said 'it' or 'thingy'. I was just used to saying 'cock', which was what they said at school, 'round the back', and which made it worse to have to undress for Aunt Maud to look at it. It is enough now to leave myself sitting in the old zinc bath in the scullery, when the water was soothing, and my cock was hidden, and I was hoping Aunt Maud would go back into the living room before Mum told me to stand up to be dried.

CHAPTER 3

Sycamore trees in summer made shadows in front of the 'little school', which was for infants and juniors. On my first day at school, I was brought by Hazel Barrett who lived next door to us with Mrs Sturman and held my hand to bring me and took my scared feelings away. Hazel was several years older than me. She was already in the 'big school'.

My first memory of school is of the day I rubbed some plasticene into my hair, instead of rolling it in my hands to shape letters, as we were taught to do. I didn't know that it would not pull out easily, so I was suddenly very worried, and when someone opened the door I ran out, to go home. Then I heard shouting, and two big boys were chasing me. When they caught me, they dragged me back, and I sat in my desk and cried, while 'Miss' tried to get the bits out of my hair.

To the left of the trees, as you looked towards the school, was a play area of grass, which separated Mrs Hart's school from the 'big school' of her husband. Really, he was head of both, and in winter he spent a long time sitting on the fireguard of the open fire in the little school when he wanted some time away from his own classroom. Once, he sent someone to fetch 'the stick' from the big school, so he could cane some of us in front of the class, before he sat back We thought the teachers were almost as scared of him as we were. When Hart was not there, the little school could be quite a happy place.

A dark green curtain was pulled forward much of the time to separate infants and juniors. You could hear the usual classroom noises from the other end, in particular when Mrs Hart raised her voice to tell someone off, or when someone knocked over a stack of equipment stored behind a low curtain at the side of the infants' end. In Miss Stevenson's class, one of the punishments was to be made to stand in a corner or facing the wall at the front of the class. Sometimes, when someone cried because their punishment was not fair, usually because someone else had avoided being found out, Miss Stevenson made them fetch an empty jam jar from the cupboard to catch tears in.

Some of the best times were when the green curtain was pulled back for country dancing. Mrs Hart put a record on the gramophone. In this way we were taught to enjoy some tunes and dances with odd names we never knew the meaning of, like Selenger's Round, making the boards bounce under our efforts. Some of the songs had daft words: 'If all the world was paper / And all the seas were ink / If all the trees were bread and cheese / What would we have to drink?'

We were called 'the little'ns'. Mrs Hart's class were 'the big'ns' The teachers said 'the little ones' and 'the big ones'. We were five or six, they were seven, eight, or nine. The real 'big'ns' were in the big school, which was near the church.

We called it 'going round the back'. There was a row of four privies, two for boys, two for girls, divided by a wooden partition. In front of these was 'the boy's', a corrugated-iron place to pee in, painted red outside, unpainted inside. We peed against the tinny wall and it drummed with the sound. Sometimes, someone climbed up on the top wooden rail ,which was there to hold the place together, and peed down. He could be seen from all around, the girls in their places laughing and encouraging, and at the same time accusing him of looking into where they should be private. Nobody ever seemed to tell any of this to the teachers, so everybody was able to go on enjoying the rudeness.

When we needed a drink, there was a pail of water in the lobby, where we hung our coats. There was only one mug for all of us to use. It was old and battered, with the white enamel chipped all over. The same pail of water stayed there in the left hand corner by the door all day.

Miss Stevenson sometimes brought a girl to school, when she had her to stay for a while in her home. She wore a black gymslip, which was unlike the way all the other girls were dressed. She had dark hair, dark eyes, and she was good to look at. I always liked the times when she was there. She was one of the best things that happened at school. Some people are better to be with than others, and she was one of them. Miss Stevenson was her aunt, but there was no family likeness at all, the aunt pale and light haired, with pale eyes.

There was another girl in Miss Stevenson's class who had something called St Vitus' dance, which made her unable to keep still. We each had a little blackboard for writing on with chalk. It was used every day for learning words. Edith's board got smaller and smaller because she chewed it at the corners. It became so small that there was no room for writing. Soon, it had gone, and Miss Stevenson gave her a new one. People said that she was sometimes tied to the washing-mangle at home, so her mother could get on with the housework.

At the end of Miss Stevenson's part of the schoolroom, there was a long, wide shelf, low down, with a curtain hanging from it. The curtain was kept closed. When you first went to school, you wondered what was behind it. One day someone touched against the curtain and some deckchairs crashed out. Miss Stevenson laid them on their sides again and pushed them back. Now we knew what was there, but we were always afraid to be the one who might knock them down next time, because Miss Stevenson would 'go mad'. When my cousin Russell came to live with us for a few weeks while Uncle George was very ill after a motorbike accident, he came to school with me. Later, the main thing he remembered about that time was the deckchairs falling out.

A glass bowl for goldfish was on the top of the piano at the front of the classroom, just into Mrs Hart's end, as you came in from the lobby. The green curtain didn't quite reach to there, so all of us could see. But there were no goldfish going round and round, just tadpoles, waggling tails and wriggling everywhere. Someone had brought us frogspawn, for us to watch them grow and change. We liked to look, to see them growing day by day. We weren't allowed to talk much to each other, but had to 'get on with your work' or ,when 'Miss' was talking, listen, keep your eyes on her, not look away at tadpoles or at anything, except the things she pointed to, just on the blackboard usually.

It happened one weekend, when nobody was there to see. The top of the piano had been left folded back, the way they sometimes are. The tadpole bowl could still stand there. Sometime, in the dark, perhaps, some tadpoles had finished changing into frogs, were hopping everywhere, over the piano, off it to the floor, but mostly to inside. We weren't tall enough to see them there, but you could hear, and see them by imagining. If you knew what a piano was like inside, it was easier. 'All them wires', we thought. You could imagine tiny sounds, perhaps, the dark in there, and frogs more than there really were. And tell it at home, the moment you got there, the first thing you had to tell, and it was only once. We didn't have tadpoles the next year.

There was a blind man who used to go round schools and homes, to tune pianos. We didn't have one, but there was one at Sunnyside. Someone said he didn't need to see because his ears were so very, very good at hearing how a music note should be. I tried to imagine that, but couldn't. And I can't remember if the blind man came to tune our piano at the little school after the frogs, and water from them, got inside.

Perhaps it was when I first saw him. Or is it my imagining puts him there?

In Mrs Hart's end, some teaching was at her desk, when children stood in a circle and took their turn at reading from their copy of the book. Sometimes, she slapped fingers with her ruler if a mistake was made. One book I truly loved was *Gypsy Dick.* I liked the boy, and liked to be him, moving on to somewhere else. Mrs Hart's best lessons were history and geography. Often, for these, she sat on the front children's desk, with her feet on the seat. Some children said they could see her knickers when she sat in this position, but whether this was true was not sure. Certainly, she managed to keep everyone looking to her face, because what she said was interesting, and everyone was too scared to be caught out talking rude. Her face was redder than most people's and even redder when she was angry.

When Mrs Hart mentioned the story of the Flood and Noah's Ark, you would think of it happening outside the school windows, which were so high that we couldn't see out, except to the trees and sky. The water would get higher and higher up the walls, which, inside, were painted shiny brown, the shape of bricks still clear, to just above our heads, with a creamy colour upwards from there, all dull with dampness often in the wintertime, except where our clothes could brush. It was harder to think about the animals than the rising water, except for those we knew. The wood Noah used for planks, Dad cut on the saw bench in the foundry yard. It wasn't gopher wood, but ash and willow, poplar too. Mount Ararat was hazy, in the sky, past Diss. The dove came down on Ashton's red roof tiles.

We learned to act a play, and people came to see us in the Village Hall. I have forgotten what it was about because I wanted to forget about it. There was a part in it in which you had to say too much to remember. You had to stand at the front of the stage and speak straight to the audience. I was remembering the words very well, then suddenly there were no more in my head. I stopped speaking and looked across the people's faces into the dark, and still the words didn't come. Mrs Hart was sitting at the piano, on the floor just below the left-hand end of the stage. I looked at her and said the only thing I could think of.

'Please, Miss, I don't know any more.' And the audience gave the biggest laugh of the evening.

In summer, caterpillars came on the hawthorn hedge along the edge of the stony little road towards the 'big school'. They were bright orange and black, furry, and easy to have on your hand. I didn't know which kind of butterflies they changed into, because we never happened to be there when they changed. Perhaps it was into moths anyway.

Just beyond the end of the hedge, there was a tiny white-boarded sweet shop, run by Mrs Thrower, whose house stood back behind a garden. Mrs Thrower knew which sweets were most likely to be wanted, so had a few jars of them and not much else. Aniseed balls were favourites. To make them last, we folded them into a handkerchief, if we had one, and sucked through that. After Mrs Thrower left, there was Mrs Skipper

My name was meant to come from the blade of my penknife on to the windowsill outside the lobby, but just as I started, with my head down, so keen to do it well, a hard clout came on my right ear. Hart was riled, but didn't need to say much, and afterwards I was amazed to think how I had dared to try anything so daft, because my name would have been there to show who 'done it'. My ear, and the side of my face, felt tender for days.

a⅍

Mrs Hart often brought her little dog called Bobby. She had to spend much of her time calling him to her, scolding him, always being watchful for his bad habits. The main one was his liking for clinging his front legs round one of ours and rubbing his belly against it. However many times she brought him to school, he never learned how to behave, like some children she had to tell off. Under the desks, we kicked him away, but he always came back.

CHAPTER 4

Uncle Dick's butcher's shop was at the far
end of the Green, where the road went off
to New Buckenham. It was always scrubbed
inside, painted white outside, with a large
window, and a door that had top and bottom
halves that could open or close separately. The
bare wood floor was covered in very clean
sawdust, and no blood spills were allowed to
stay on it. But there was always the smell of raw
meat, and Uncle Dick's hands gathered smears
of blood, and looked cold from the handling.
His knife slid expertly into the red lumps, and
bones splintered under the chop of his little
axe. After he had cut off a customer's piece of
meat or string of sausages, he wiped his hands
on a muslin cloth. Then he put a hand up to
where there was a pencil, safe behind the top
of his right ear, against his dark curly hair. He
would write a bill on a little pad, tear it off,

and fix it on the paper wrapping. Any man who had to use a pencil in his job would be likely to use his ear like that, and the pencil never seemed to fall out. But it always fell when I tried it.

When there were no customers left, Uncle Dick let me follow him out to the cupboard with a zinc-filled door, fixed on the back wall of the building. Here, the smell of meat was unpleasant, and white maggots could be seen if you dared to look. Uncle Dick's greyhounds were always eager for the sound of his coming, and his ferrets squeaked their evil-sounding pleasure. But that daily end of the story was a mile away from the bright shop at the edge of the Green. It was at the little farm at Stacksford, which has its own sad story I shall not think about here. Instead, here is a good memory.

One wintry evening, Uncle Dick took me in his pony trap with gentle Dinah pulling us, for late deliveries of meat, on Christmas Eve. Clip-clop of trotting hooves was real, the long whip too, but never used, for this was love of man and horse, the boy there for the ride, drawn close, warm-blanketed, with reins to hold, to learn from, easily.

George Jolly drove his horse and cart out of Uncle Harry's yard, came past the foundry and the blacksmith's, and turned into Rod Alley Row. He stopped to deliver to Mrs Moore, led the horse along, leaving it to stand obediently as he went to each house, mostly going round the back to each, with his basket on his arm. The basket was woven of almost white osiers (or something of that kind), and the bread would still be warm. At our house, there was no way round to the back, as there was the extra part built on for my great-grandfather's big family, but there was a second front door, up the yard past the May tree. George didn't knock but went straight in. If he found nobody inside, he would leave the loaf on the table. The door was always left unlocked, so the regular callers never had to wait for someone to open it.

It always gave me a proud feeling to know that Uncle Harry's bread went into so many houses, not only in this village but also in outlying places. George and several other men had helped to make the bread earlier this morning. The delivery had been by horse and cart for very many years, but now Uncle Stephen, Uncle Harry's son, had a van.

Mrs Hart told us 'Bread is the staff of life', and that made it sound very important, even before she explained why it was compared to a staff. You felt good because you knew you had plenty of bread, and it was good to know that some of the best wheat in the world was grown in Norfolk, and some of it was threshed by H E Loveday and Sons, and that Grandad said that his machines threshed better than anyone else's.

When Mum cut one of Uncle Harry's loaves, each piece was called a 'round'. I didn't know why. It would have made more sense if the loaf had been round, but every loaf had two sides and two ends, and was just slightly rounded at the top. She always cut the rounds in half as soon as the butter was on. People I thought posh usually cut their rounds from corner to corner, to make triangles. That was one of the signs of being posh.

This bread I carry home, still warm in paper wrap, it smells so good, good, good, my fingers poke and pinch its perfect golden edges, almost guiltlessly. She never says a word.

We went down Gypsy Lane. We knew there would be no gypsies now. The name was old. In olden days, they must have come quite often, stopping there a while. So we excited ourselves with imagining the long ago. The hedges had grown high on either side, with the worn- smooth earthen path between, with grass and weeds on both sides too. It curved away, so there was just a chance that one day there might be gypsies back again, just out of sight, beyond the bend. It was a good place, anyway, for blackberries, and for knowing there were no eyes watching us. So when we were on our way to Stacksford or the warren, we might go down Gypsy Lane and come out at the other end, on to the road that crossed the Stacksford road a short way down. Sometimes, we even stayed in Gypsy Lane instead of going where we had set out to go.

I went about singing bits of 'Play to Me Gypsy', which lots of people were singing as they walked or biked or drove their horse and cart. All the words were in my head, and it was the best song I knew.

Oh play to me gypsy,
The moon's high above,
Oh play me your melody,
That song I love.

Beside your caravan
The camp fire's bright,
I'll be your vagabond
Just for tonight.

I must have heard it for the first time on the wireless at Sunnyside, but soon everybody seemed to know it. It made pictures in your head of caravans under moonlight, the sound of violins or guitars, or mouth-organs, men singing to young women, or young women singing to men, and you imagined what it was like to be them. You could almost feel you were with them, or were them, but without the nervousness of not knowing what to do. I knew it all the way through. There were some words that seemed special. Sometimes, people changed the words slightly, singing 'serenade' in place of 'melody'. 'Vagabond' sounded exciting and strange, different from the word we were used to hearing, when someone might say, 'You little vagabond' and mean something like 'You little ragamuffin', both of which were said if you were untidy or your clothes were torn.

A very usual sound when someone came towards you, was singing. Some men whistled tunes. I tried to whistle, but could never manage to make more than two notes. I sang, but only to myself. I got to know the words very easily, but didn't dare to sing out because my voice didn't sound good enough. In church or school, I only pretended to sing by opening and closing my lips in the right way, but no sound came out. Nobody seemed to notice, but I couldn't be sure.

People who sang most, out on the roads or somewhere at work, were moving along, like Uncle Dick in his pony trap, or George Jolly on his bread rounds, and men on bikes. Ladies sang as they used their yellow dusters, or looked after children, especially babies. It was nice to hear them sing lullabies. You seemed to be able to remember it being done for you, as it had been, over and over, 'Hush-a-bye, baby, in the tree top', and all that stuff from long ago.

The first song I could remember Dad singing was 'My Blue Heaven'. He sang it quietly to himself sometimes, and I got to know the words a bit. Sometimes he played it on his mouth-organ and I thought of the words as he played. It was a happy song, and it seemed to be about a happy place somewhere Dad could imagine that was not meant to be true but just a place you could go to in your imagination and believe to be true while the singing or the music lasted. I didn't think that out, but that's how it felt.

When whippoorwills call and evening is nigh,
I hurry to my blue heaven.
A turn to the right and a little white light
Will lead you to my blue heaven.
A smiling face; a fireplace, a cosy room,
A little nest that nestles where the roses bloom,
With Molly and me, and baby makes three,
We're happy in my blue heaven.

Dad also sang 'Two Little Girls in Blue' and another one from which they took my sister Thora's name. It was called 'Speak to me Thora'. I heard it on a gramophone record and didn't like it much. When we said we didn't like something much, it really meant we didn't like it at all, but that was not usually about songs. The song I truly liked, or loved, really, was 'Play to Me Gypsy'. None of the people who sang as they worked had many songs. They simply liked their few songs coming back time after time, filling their days with feelings it was good to have. And they made everybody's days better, even if nobody ever told them.

CHAPTER 5

Iwas in Elvin's Yard with Reggie, near the back door. I think there was only one door, so it was the front door too. Mrs Elvin came out with a tin of shortcakes, and gave us one each. She seemed to know I liked shortcakes. Hers were very good, almost as good as my mother's.

A very old woman called Biah lived near Elvin's yard. The only place she was ever seen was on the road that went past Aunt Gee's shop, the foundry, and the blacksmith's, to the Post Office. My sister Thora, when tiny, was terrified of her for no reason anybody could understand. It could have been only Biah's strange appearance, clothes all long and black, very white face, old-fashioned hat. Thora called her 'Ol' lor' lady', and ran away if she saw her, even in the distance, calling out the name. We never knew who had frightened her with the thought of 'Lord', or why old Biah brought that idea back to her.

Often, old ladies were called 'old crones'. It seemed a funny word, but also a bit frightening. Mum would say that an old man or woman was 'a bit doddery'.

The taste of shortcakes my mother made was the best taste I knew. She made her dough with flour and milk and a bit of butter, and kneaded it with very clean hands that she kept sprinkling with flour so the dough didn't stick to them. Then she rolled the dough with the rolling pin on the baking board till it was flattened into a patch of pastry that nearly covered the board. It was about as thick as a finger. Next she got a handful of currants out of their paper bag and sprinkled them over half the pastry, then sprinkled on sugar before folding the other half back over. The next thing to do was to cut that lot in halves and put one half on top of the other, with more currants and a good sprinkle of sugar in between. Now came the cutting into cake shapes, by a knife if they were to be square, or by a cutter shaped to make them round when she pressed it down. Lastly, she would dip her pastry brush into a cup of raw egg she had 'whisked up', and spread it over the cakes so they would be light brown and shiny when they came out of the oven. The best part was about half-an-hour later, the lovely smell when the oven door was opened and Mum took them out on their tray.

On the same afternoon, which was usually Friday, she would make jam tarts, cheese straws, and coconut pyramids, and, occasionally, a jam Swiss-roll.

Over the well, Dad had built a wooden structure shaped like a roof, to hold the roller on which the long chain was wound to raise the water pail. Two small doors, side by side, were kept closed when the well was not in use. The pail was held by a clip, and moved by turning the handle on the right hand side. It was always a slightly frightening moment when I opened the doors and looked in. The water was a long way down. In my head was the strict caution my mother always gave. As the pail reached the surface, it usually tipped on its side and sank. There was a temptation to go on turning the handle until the pail was likely to be on the bottom, but usually thoughts of what the bottom might be covered by, the bones of creatures that had fallen in during all the years before the well was properly covered, were enough to stop me from doing anything beyond my mother's instructions. Raising the pail and taking it off the chain had to be done carefully, and it would have been unlikely that anyone could ever be a regular drawer of water without the experience of losing control of the handle and having the roller race round, unwinding the chain and letting the full pail crash down. In the scullery, the pail was kept under the sink and the water was used as sparingly as possible because of the bother of bringing it there. It was our drinking water.

The roller towel hung on the door, the scullery door out to 'the back', which was the garden, privy, gate, the orchard, and the foundry yard. The iron latch was halfway up the left-hand side, unpainted, just plain iron to our hands, and old. The towel edge just missed it as it moved. How easily that roller rolled! It had been rolling every day since it was put there in 'Victorian times'. The towel went in the copper every Monday morning wash, to have the dirt boiled out, the whiteness back, and then the faded pattern on the edges ironed so smooth and welcoming.

We all used it. Dad 'cleaned up' when he came in from work, and never came through to the living room till all the oil, or grease, or dust, or rust was gone. Mum used it when she turned from 'messy' jobs to clean ones. I used it when I came for meals, or after 'going up the yard'. It got too wet: you pulled it down to find a dry, or drier, part. You rolled it past the grubby marks 'someone-in-a-hurry' made, and tried to leave none of your own. On school days, Mum reminded, 'Wash your face,' or grabbed you as you turned away, and wiped the flannel round your mouth.

'A lick and a promise,' she would say. I was not quite sure what it meant, and didn't wonder much. But I liked her saying it.

The click of the latch on the back door meant Dad was home. After a call from the scullery, he would take off his dusty clothes and wash quickly at the sink before coming through to the living room where we waited, ready to eat. Mum would be moving about between pantry, cooking range, and scullery.

Dad crossed the hearth to his chair on the right hand side. He was wearing his long pants, 'long johns', or was waiting for Mum to bring clean ones, or a clean shirt from the wooden 'clothes horse' near the cooking range. His dressing was always in the same order – long shirt tucked down after sitting to pull on his trousers, buttoning his shirt, fixing sleeves and cuffs, asking 'Kath', to find his collar stud, which usually happened to be upstairs.

The meal was from the cooking range, vegetables from steaming saucepans, pie from the oven. There was talk, about work, about home, about the village. Meals always followed a pattern given by the day of the week, Monday, cold meat and hot vegetables, Tuesday, shepherd's pie, to finish the Sunday joint, Wednesday and Thursday, sausages or other meat dishes, and Fridays, fish, because there was a regular delivery van.

When we occasionally had chicken, there was one part that nobody wanted to eat. Mum said it was called 'the parson's nose', and she asked who would like it, but anyone could see it was the chicken's bum. The Reverend Henry Anderson was our parson. He was called 'the Vicar' or just 'Old Henry Anderson'. He had been the vicar for a long time. His nose was not pointed or turned-up, like a chicken's bum, but was quite big, with ginger hairs in it, and a little bit red.

We loved saying a rhyme my mother told: 'One, two, three, Mother caught a flea, / Put it in the teapot and made a pot of tea, / The flea jumped out, hit her on the snout, / In came Father with his shirt hanging out.' We thought of the father running out of a privy.

A few weeks before Christmas, Aunt Gee turned her living room into part of the shop, for display of Christmas goods. Nobody was serving in there, so anything you wanted to buy had to be taken through to the shop counter. When I was seven or eight, I realized that it would be quite easy to take a sugar mouse (pink or white) without paying, which is what I did. I had never known before that day how guilty it was possible to feel after stealing something so cheap.

Wellingtons were good in snow. We wore two pairs of socks, but still your feet got cold. Cold was better, though, than wet. Snow went through your leather boots much quicker than the rain. You couldn't put the dubbin on to keep it out, as we did on football boots. If you did, they would never shine again. So we wore our wellingtons and got cold toes. They ached, as they thawed out, just as your fingers did. You shook your hands like mad, both together, out in from of you, your fingers spread, each hand pointing at the other, shake, shake, shake, till they came warm, but, oh, they ached.

Just under our cold knees, at front and sides, our legs were chafed by wellingtons. However long your socks might be, they still slipped down. If your mother made you garters from her white elastic, sometimes it worked, but if your socks stayed up, the garters often were too tight. You had a painful ring, your skin all crinkled up. We put up with the chafing, mostly. She put on Vaseline or Germoline. The chafe felt hot, her finger cold.

The snow, the snow is falling, snow, snow, snow, on everything, on me, my face turned up, my eyelids, lips, my nose, now open eyes. Across the Green there's nothing any more, no trees the other side, no paths, no goalposts, no one walking. Turn a bit, the oak tree halfway up, beside the road that disappears, the willows further left, the ash, just there enough to see, anyone walking would be a ghost. A moving light, two lights come through, bigger, bigger, bigger, slowly, he can't see, comes down, and past, and gone, and almost silently. The fire indoors, go in, come in, she's telling me.

Someone gave Thora a little black kitten with white paws. She called it Tissy. It always wanted to be playful. Its favourite game was pouncing on something, which was usually something that would be pulled away. The pulling away made the game much better, and Tissy never gave up. The favourite thing to pounce on was a length of string or wool. But that was in the game. Not in the game, was something we discovered when Tissy pounced on Thora's toes at bedtime. What she wanted to do was suck them, so we had to start being careful not to take off socks when she was watching. We soon discovered that whenever shoes were taken off she was watching, ready. She soon learned that socks got holes in them. A hole big enough for the tip of a toe to show was enough. Mum said that Tissy had been taken from her mother too soon. Perhaps she said, 'Poor little mite.' She often said it about children. After we went to bed she might do her 'darning', which was mending holes with wool, usually in socks.

'It gets on my wick,' Mum said. I didn't know what made her say that, because I hadn't been listening to what anyone was saying, with my 'head stuck in a book'. But people said that when they were 'fed up' with something someone did. I thought of the wick in the lamp on the table. It was called an oil lamp because it had to have paraffin oil in the round part made of brass, through the little opening under its tightly screwed-up cap. The wick dipped down into the oil, like the stringy wick of a candle in its wax, but it was flat, and as wide as two of my fingers. When Mum or Dad took the glass part off the lamp, and struck a match, and put it to the wick, a flame came on the wick because of the oil it had drawn up. When the glass was on again, it was good to watch as it steadily burned yellow, with little touches of blue at the bottom, and lit up the room and the tablecloth and our faces, and made shadow on the turned-away sides of faces, and on us or the walls when we moved, and left the corners of the room in darkness, and corners of the ceiling too, and one big spread of yellowish white in the middle. Sometimes, we made shadow shapes by holding our hands between the lamp and the ceiling or the nearest wall or the pages of a book.

What got on Mum's wick most was when people did a stupid thing 'over and over again'.

If someone cried a lot, we would say he was 'always howling' or 'a-howling'. If it went on and on, we could say, 'He howled his eyes out.'

If it was sudden, like when someone was hit, you might say he bawled. If we didn't know why someone was crying, we might ask what they were 'blahing for'. When we asked that, it might be because we thought they were 'putting on their parts', which was what grown-ups said when they didn't think we really needed to cry. So you didn't want to blah if you were sensible. Sometimes you tried not to cry, but it just came anyway. If Mum was telling about someone crying, she might say they *piped their eye*. Posh people, and people in books and newspapers, wept. What we did most was grizzle

We got worms. Until then, we thought worms were just the pale red things that slid and squiggled through the ground, but one day your mother said something that surprised you. 'You've got worms!' She thought you'd got them because you were scratching your bum, and that was 'a sign'. In a few days, you would see them for the first time, and you would not be able to think 'No, I haven't' any more. They were there, squiggling inside your poo, like tiny bits of white cotton, twisting about like mad, as if they were wondering what was happening, out of the dark inside you, into the light, and not liking it. But you would feel glad they were out, and horrified that they had been inside you.

'Must have been that rhubarb,' Mum said.

There were several things they could come from. It seemed mysterious, but everybody could expect to get them sometime, because it was part of nature. It made you wonder about being part of nature. But you got used to children having worms because your friends had them too, not often, but enough to be part of nature.

Then somebody told you it was possible to have a tapeworm, which was much worse. No, you should not worry about tapeworms, because they came mainly in animals. Dogs had them. So did horses. They had their name because they were like long pieces of white tape going up through the winding guts. Even their heads were flat. They might live inside the poor animal for ages. So then you understood something you had heard long ago, somebody saying a new puppy needed to be 'wormed', which was done by having some powder put on his food to make the worms come out 'at the other end'.

One day, Uncle Dick's lovely, gentle horse, Dinah, was gone, and he was driving a blue van, singing to himself, but loudly, as he came down the Green. He was singing out of the wide open window, and now was not only singing to himself but to amuse me as he passed. He would sing all the way home, where the van would turn on to the grass at the far end of the Rod Alley pit.

CHAPTER 6

'Someone,' said Mrs Hart, '*someone* has made an odour'.

She said it often. We put our heads down, but still tried to see Mrs Hart's face. We didn't want to 'catch her eye', because that would be a sure way of letting her think we were the guilty one, and say our name. She sometimes said a name anyway, like 'Charlie Large' (but she would say 'Charles'). She might make a guess, and we might think she was right or wrong, but it wasn't us, anyway, and we could feel safe as long as we didn't catch her eye. We could have said it was her Bobby, but nobody would dare. Sometimes we knew who it was, but nobody ever said.

Mrs Hart told us good stories from history. She didn't read them from a book but told them from her own memories of someone, like her teacher, telling them to her. She had got some of them from books, but they always had her own feelings in them. There were many stories but those I remember first are of Horatio Nelson. He was a Norfolk boy. It was good for a Norfolk boy to learn that. We could see the North Sea that he saw, unchanged. We could imagine him at twelve years, three or four years older than us, on his first ship, a midshipman, an officer from the start, even if he was only learning the job, imagine the strangeness of it, the new things to learn, having to grow up quickly, venture forth, like on the polar ice, the polar bear ready to attack, attacking. Level the rifle. Fire! Look at that great creature dead, sailors coming over the ice, leading, back to the safety of the ship, the talk, the talk. 'Did you not feel fear?' 'What is fear?' Years later, battle soon, the Spanish fleet, beware, beware, the telescope to his blind eye, his way of doing as he must, 'I see no Spanish ships.'

She told the story of another Norfolk person, Nurse Edith Cavell, who had lived at Swardeston, where her father was the vicar, and where my Aunt Maud and Uncle Harold now lived. She was a nurse in the Great War, caring for wounded British soldiers in Belgium. When the German army defeated Belgium, she nursed German soldiers too. But she also secretly helped British soldiers to escape back to Britain. The Germans discovered what she was doing, and ordered her to be shot by a firing-squad. Before she was shot, she spoke some words that became famous all over the world and will always be remembered. 'Now I know that patriotism is not enough. I must bear no ill will to anyone.'

Mrs Hart had a favourite from the time he started school. From his first day in Miss Stevenson's class he was called 'Charles MacDonald' though he was really Charles MacDonald Large. Mrs Hart said we should all say 'Charles MacDonald' because there was already a Charles Large in the class. We soon knew Charles MacDonald was her favourite because she was always saying his name, and always kindly. It was as if everything he did pleased her. Usually, when she said someone's name a lot, it meant the opposite. We said 'Charlie Mac'. He was a nice boy. So was Charlie Large. I always wished I was as good as he was at football. We called him Billy.

In a corner at the front of Mrs Hart's class, behind the blackboard-and- easel, was a small table, and on the table there were sometimes model 'scenes' showing places in the world. For a while there was a desert, with sand, and palm trees we made from paper. The best scene was a Japanese garden. The grass of the garden was moss. In the moss there was a space made for a lake, and the lake was a piece of glass from a broken mirror. There were trees made from twigs stuck in plasticene, which made mounds under the moss. A wooden bridge of matchsticks went over a stream of glass, and a narrow path led to it, and away on the other side. A few coloured paper lanterns hung in low branches, and a few small Japanese figures, the ladies in kimonos, stood on the path or crossed the grass. It was a little magic place we helped to make and would never forget. It stayed there quite a long while. I thought of it at home and made an imitation on an old tin tray.

The saddest story Mrs Hart told us was about Captain Scott. He led a party of explorers to the Antarctic, starting in 1910, to study the area that had never been explored, but also to be the first people to reach the South Pole. But they didn't reach the Pole until January 1912, and then found that a Norwegian party, led by Amundsen, had got there five weeks before.

Captain Scott's party was of only five men, because others had been sent back when horses had to be shot because they couldn't manage to go any further in the snow, and also because teams of dogs were not needed for the last stage of the journey.

When Scott, Oates, Evans, Wilson, and Bowers were on their way back, there was terrible weather. Evans became ill, and died.

Captain Oates had bad frost-bite in his feet, which was made worse by an old war wound. Captain Scott wrote in his diary that Captain Oates had said to him, 'I'm just going outside, and I may be some time.' I could see a picture in my mind, of a figure stumbling away in the snow, and new snow falling, so he becomes invisible, so what happens is never known, except we know that he knew he would not be coming back because his friends could travel better without him.

But they didn't travel well. The weather was too bad. Scott's last words in his diary were, 'Take care of our people.' It was found by a search party. They buried the three bodies under their tent, which would soon be deep under the snow.

There was one of Mrs Hart's stories that came back to me over and over, and gave a feeling of wanting it to end differently, even though I knew it never could. It was the story of Joan of Arc. When it got to the part about her being burnt at the stake, the thought came as a wish that the men at her trial could still come to a different judgement.

❧

'Last night you sleep-walked,' my mother said. 'I heard you coming down the stairs. I opened the staircase door, and there you were. "What do you want?" I said. You didn't look at me. Your eyes were open. You just stepped down and went past me as if I wasn't there, went round the table to the scullery door, went in the scullery, and I followed you. You went over to the sink, reached out to the face flannel, opened it, and blew your nose, and put the flannel back, still sound asleep. Then you turned, and went the way you came. You climbed the stairs. I followed you, in case you fell. You pattered along the landing to the little bedroom, got into bed, and went off sound asleep. I tucked you in, and you hadn't known a thing about it all. Can you remember anything?' The only thing I knew was what she'd just said. Every time she told it after that, it stayed the same.

CHAPTER 7

I wished my name had been Rupert. I didn't tell many people that, and soon grew out of wishing it. The name seemed good because of Rupert Bear, and Prince Rupert, the Cavalier. Afterwards, it seemed a daft idea and I felt foolish for wishing it. Plain 'John' became good enough, and 'Honest John' was even better. Long John Silver was an exciting connection. 'Little John' was fine when it wasn't me. John the Baptist I didn't like at all.

It gave me a good feeling when someone I didn't know very well called me 'John'. But when people asked me my name and I told them 'John Loveday', some would say, 'Oh, you're Tom's boy'. Occasionally, someone who only knew my family name would call me 'Young Tom'.

'Rats! They fought the dogs and killed the cats...' The children of New Buckenham acted the story of the poem 'The Pied Piper of Hamelin' which was supposed to have happened in Germany, hundreds of years ago. The place had a plague of rats.

The mayor and corporation had to find a way of getting rid of them. The Pied Piper, a man strangely dressed, in clothes of red and yellow, appeared in the town He said he could rid them of the rats for a fee of 'a thousand guilders'. The mayor said 'A thousand! I'll give fifty!' (meaning, fifty thousand.) The agreement was made, and the Pied Piper went out and started to play his pipe. Straight away, rats began to run towards him, and followed as he walked away.

Dad and Mum took us to watch the story acted in the ruins of the castle just outside New Buckenham. It still had a moat, which was 'the river Weser, deep and wide' to which the Piper led the scampering rats. We didn't see the drowning because the spectators were asked not to follow. The moat was not very deep or wide, but it looked deep because of the dark trees. We had to imagine every rat jumping into the water and being drowned, because the children could not be quite realistic at this point, and anyway, they were needed for the rest of the performance, after a change of costume.

In the story, when the Pied Piper went to get his reward of a thousand guilders, the Mayor wouldn't keep his promise now the rats had gone. The Piper's revenge soon came. He went out and began to play. As he walked, the children of Hamelin came out of the houses and began to follow, happy under the spell of the music. The children of New Buckenham, who had crept back among the castle ruins and changed from being rats to being the happy children of Hamelin, followed the Piper wherever he went. When all were there, he went towards a high mountain, which we had to imagine. In the story, a great cavern opened in the side of the mountain and the Piper went in, the children following. The people of Hamelin looked on helplessly, and the people who had come to watch the acting could stand and imagine what those other people must have felt. The children acting were hidden somewhere behind the castle walls. Those of Hamelin were in the mountain, except for one. He was lame, and couldn't keep up with the rest, and the mountain closed as he tried to follow the music into the wonderful place it seemed to promise. The poem tells how he sadly talked of it always, and of his friends.

The children running from gaps in the old walls to follow the Piper was the best part, both as scampering rats or happy Hamelin children. The poem was one I had heard from Mum, so I knew some bits by heart. It was good to know them as a man read them out.

When my sister Barbara was still small enough to be in a pram, I 'took her for a walk', with Thora walking at the side. Before we had gone only halfway round the Green two children had 'latched on' to us. One was Reggie Elvin. We walked on happily, and when we came to the Grange corner, turned down towards the mill. We went on past the mill, and knew that now we were going to the warren, without even a thought about whether it was too far to take the baby in her pram. We came to the warren turning off the Stacksford road and went up there. On the warren, it was fun, and we went off the road and over the heather, somehow, till we found a gateway closed, next to a field. There was a ditch, with a grassy bank sloping down to it. Somehow, the pram slipped down, and we were looking at it, with Barbara looking up at us. Suddenly, we were scared, and knew we'd come too far. Nobody was to blame, because we hadn't thought, or even talked and planned. We were just there.

Reggie was good at knowing what to do. We got the pram up after a while, and it seemed late, so we set off for home. That part of the warren seemed a long way from the road. And when we reached the road it seemed still far from home. Everywhere looked different, even the road itself. A man was coming on a bicycle. When he was near we called to him, to ask how to get home. As he passed, he told us, 'The way you came,' and he was gone. We went the way he'd come from, on and on, and then there was someone calling us, and glad to see us. People were searching everywhere, down all the roads away from the Green. I can't remember getting home, except for Mum saying about the people searching everywhere.

I never took Barbara for a walk again.

Whenever we did something we shouldn't do, we wondered if we would be found out. The trouble that came was called 'getting wrong'. 'You'll get wrong for that,' someone might say, and it often happened that we did. 'Getting wrong' was getting told off, and sometimes punished in some way, like sent to bed, kept indoors, forbidden to do something, made to wait, not given an expected present. 'Did you get wrong?' your friends might ask. 'No, I never,' you would say. You sometimes said 'No, I never' when you had got wrong. It sounded as if you didn't like to admit it, which was true. I didn't get wrong much, because my mother seemed to know how things happened. She knew a lot of wise old sayings that seemed to cover so many mistakes that we made. 'Sticks and stones can break my bones, but words will never hurt me'. 'Take it from whence it comes.' 'It's all in a day's work.' 'Who does she think she is?' 'She thinks she's Lady Muck.' 'A little kindness goes a long way.' There were many, many more.

She often knew what we had done wrong, even though she hadn't seen. 'A little dickybird told me.'

We had relatives at Tibenham, which was about two miles beyond New Buckenham. They were 'the Marshalls'. I don't know how they were related to us, but it was through the Whitehand family. Herbert Marshall was a 'gentleman farmer'. He had been an officer in the Great War, and still had his little 'officer moustache'. His farmhouse was down a long driveway, after a gate which Dad had to get out of the car to open and close. We had to call him 'Uncle Herbert', just as Mum did. But I think she was saying it so that we would copy her. Dad just said 'Herbert'. Herbert's wife was Aunt Emmy. That didn't seem a posh name and she didn't seem as posh as Herbert. They had three children, all girls. Joyce, the youngest, was younger than I was, but the other two were much older. They seemed a bit like what Mum called 'proper young women'. They both had 'tits', as we said at school. That should have made me like them, but it didn't. They seemed too posh and 'snooty'. The older one, with dark hair, and pretty, was Peggy. The other, with light brown hair and freckles, was called 'Paddy', but I think that was just the name she liked to have people use.

Most times when we visited, the older girls were busy with their own interests, and we didn't see them much. But one day I was left in the 'drawing room' with them while Uncle Herbert and Aunt Emmy took Mum and Dad somewhere else in the house or into the garden or by their tennis court, and my sisters were with Joyce. I can't remember what happened then, but I think they must have teased me somehow, 'on purpose', taking advantage of my shyness or nervousness, playing some sort of game with me, some trick on me, so I got 'riled up' and then 'let fly' at them, and got told off when the grown-ups came back to see 'what all the fuss was about'. It was the only time I had ever felt like that. Mum was embarrassed, because she couldn't understand. I can't remember Dad saying anything, but I think he must have said something to Mum when I was not nearby. For me, no Marshall house again.

There was someone who never said wrong things to me. I had a teddybear since the days I couldn't remember.

No more of him will fade away — there's no more fur to go. He changed so slow, I didn't know how he was changing till he had, and can't remember him before, and don't want to. His nose is black, his eyes are too. They look at you. He isn't sad to be just khaki cotton stuff the fur came off. He's like he was. I tell him what I know, or think, and he tells me. There's Rupert now, and sometimes I forget to tell as I used to.

'Pull my finger.' Reggie pointed it at me. I didn't know why he wanted me to pull it.

'Go on. Pull it.'

I pulled his finger, and Reggie let a fart.

CHAPTER 8

My grandmother noticed the swellings on the palms of my hands when she insisted on helping me to wash them thoroughly for tea. We were using a small zinc bowl in the kitchen sink.

'What's this?' she asked, 'and this?'

I lied quickly, not wanting her to know the cause was Hart's cane, because she might ask more questions. 'That's where I hold the handle of my scooter.'

She didn't believe me. She had guessed the true cause but did not want to embarrass me.

'Oh,' she said.

I hated my lie but there was no other way to answer. She said nothing more, but I wondered what she was thinking.

We sometimes sang: 'Mrs Brown went to town / To buy a pound of butter / Mr Hart let a fart / And blew it in the gutter.'

We imagined the story happening at the edge of Abbey Road, because Mrs Brown lived at Chattergate. We would all see it from where we stood in a low-lying, damp part of the Green, among little blue flowers that grew there every year.

If we looked a little further to the right, up that edge of the Green which led towards the church and the schools, we would see 'the pound'. It was made of heavy wooden posts and bars that were shaped like very big farm gates, arranged in a circle to shut in any stray cows or horses until their owners came for them. The only farmers allowed leave their cattle to graze on the Green were those who had bought the right to do it, so 'strays' were locked in the pound and their owners had pay for them to be let out. We loved to sit on the top bars of the pound, but were disappointed at never seeing a horse or cow inside. We thought that it must have been used long ago, like in the days of Queen Victoria. You had to think that it would be hard for an animal to be shut in there and see all the others free on the Green. The cattle now grazed all around. They could stand looking in, as if wondering about it.

Hart's suit, blue-grey and shiny, had a smell as if something had been spilt on it, unpleasant. Whenever he came into the little school, he stood in front of the fireguard, or even sat on it, but it was not the smell of scorching, nor the smell that came off our trousers when the teacher stood us near the fire because we'd peed ourselves. Mostly, there was no fire anyway, only sooty blackness. Hart's smell was a mystery, and we got used to it. It could have come off his skin, like from shaving soap or stuff he put on his yellowy purple face after he shaved it, and got on his hands. It didn't matter to us. There was more to dislike about him than his smell. We kept away from him, if we could.

In the 'little bedroom', the one small window looked out to the west, along the back garden path, past the privy, out of the gate, into the orchard, across Uncle Harry's gardens, up the fields hear the almshouses, and away to the sky. Because of the light sky in the west, summer evenings always seemed too long to be in bed early, and the hours spent trying in vain to sleep made me long to be among the children's voices in the distance. But I knew they were mostly older than me.

One of the pastimes in my bedroom was to make any dust on my windowsill rub on to the neckband of my shirt, so there would be a good excuse to ask for a clean shirt in the morning. The particular shirt on the first of these occasions was a very favourite grey one. I was very careful to make a natural-looking grubbiness, and for a while became so keen on having clean collars that I felt full of guilt at the extra work my mother had to do because of that bright evening sky. Sometimes, when she had too many jobs to do, she said, 'There's no rest for the wicked!'

The collars Grandad wore were not part of his shirt but big white, shiny attachments held in place by little gold collar-studs at back and front, with his necktie coming out from the turned-down collar part, and tied to lay on the broad stiff part that covered the middle of his chest. Always, it was worn with a waist-coat, sometimes called a 'weskit', made of the same material as his grey suit.

Aunt Violet showed me a drawing in her *Punch* magazine. Before it was printed, it was a pen and ink drawing, with sharp lines and the people in it very cleverly drawn. There was a short, stout lady, wearing an apron, in a scullery, ready to do the washing-up. In front of her was a boy of about my own age, looking at a saucer broken into several pieces on the floor. Underneath the drawing, was what she was saying.

'Broke your father's saucer, 'ave you? Now 'e'll 'ave to drink out of 'is cup.'

Aunt Violet loved imitating how the servant was speaking. It made me go round imitating it too. You had to say 'cup' in a funny way.

The Garden House was a small pub where the drink was cider, so it was often called the

Cider House. Dad took the family there, and we sat in the summer garden when the drinking guests had gone on a Saturday afternoon. The Holman family had once lived in Rod Alley Row, next to the Post Office, with children, Edward and Sylvia, of ages close to mine and Thora's. Mr Holman worked in a foundry near Attleborough and left his wife to run the pub through the midday opening time. The day I recalled specially was when I found a dark hedge at the side of the garden was parted slightly in one place. I could see through to a stream, and told my parents excitedly, amazed to learn, when they came to see, that my 'stream' was just the road we would travel on for home. It was the first time I found it possible for our eyes to tell us something quite untrue.

Dad took me with him once when he visited his Aunt Beatrice in her little house somewhere I had never been before. I didn't quite know how she was his aunt, but Beatrice was a nice and gentle lady, with shining eyes and a rosy face. She was a spinster, one without a spinning wheel, as all the others were, so the name seemed odd and silly now. Her little front room had a very dark brown piano. Dad said she gave piano lessons. There was a piano stool the pupils used. It was only once Dad took me, but there must have been some other times he went. She was kind and quiet, too ruddy to be beautiful, and not young, although her hair was dark, and slightly curled, and what she said to me, except my name, I soon forgot.

A tunnel under the fields, we said, went between the castle near New Buckenham and the old abbey which had been where Abbey Farm was now. None of us had seen anything to show the story true, but it was something we wanted to be true. It was still difficult to believe. This distance seemed too great, well over a mile, and it was not likely that spades and shovels could have taken them that far. But still we liked to believe, because we wanted it to be possible. If you thought about it, you could see dark figures moving with their lights, and hear footfalls in the soil. And people running, scared, or eager for the enemy.

One winter evening, Dad came in and brought a workman, 'Morry' Sturman with him. He was a little man, poor-looking, very friendly when I saw him sometimes in the foundry yard. (For quite a long time, I got his name wrong and nobody corrected me. I said 'Miry'.) Dad was worried. Somewhere between Wilby and home, he'd lost a ten-shilling note, which must have come out of his pocket as he biked home in the dark. He and Morry were going back to look for it with their bike-lights. They had a cup of tea, and went. A long time later, Dad came back. Morry had gone home.

I can't remember where he lived. I didn't know why he'd come all the way with Dad earlier. I thought he lived near Wilby anyway. They had searched and searched. Afterwards, and ever since, there has been the thought of how precious a ten-shilling note could be when not many of them came your way, and they were so hard-earned.

Two ten-shilling notes are worth a pound. Twelve pence, ('pennies') are worth a shilling. So are two sixpences, or four three pence pieces ('thre'penny bits'). Two shillings and sixpence are worth half-a-crown. A crown is obsolete.

This is what we learn in school. It makes up most of our 'arithmetic'. The rest of it is about numbers, numbers of things or people, or numbers on their own, or numbers with other numbers too, too many to make much sense, usually. We do multiplication, division, subtraction, addition. You can get the 'answer' right or wrong. It is much easier to get it wrong, which is what I do. For wrong you get crosses, for right it's ticks. A dog gets tics between his paws, a she-dog too, of course, a bitch; you have to concentrate, Mrs Hart gets riled, she shows you on the board, her chalk breaks and someone goes to pick it up, go back in your seat, she says, leave it, if you forget to carry one you'll get it wrong, and wrong again, so carry what you have to carry, or you'll stay in, stay in until you get it right, do you hear me?

'I hope you're not telling me an untruth.' Mrs Hart often said one of us had told 'an untruth'. She meant a lie. I thought she didn't like to say 'lie' because she disliked lies so much that even the word for them was something she didn't want to say. But 'untruth' was a good word because it seemed just right for the times when we said something that was not quite true but was not as bad as a big lie. She didn't explain that, but I 'worked it out'.

So we went on telling an untruth if it 'just slipped out', but mostly we kept away from lies.

'You have to have the guts to do something, sometimes,' Uncle Dick said. He looked straight at me. 'Don't let your mother think she had a jibber.'

People were always saying their wise things

'When my ship comes in,' Mum said. She often said it when she was telling you she couldn't afford to buy something. It could be something she knew you wanted. You knew it was just a way of showing she understood how much you wanted it, and she would like to be able to buy it. And a ship would be there in my head, with the grey ocean all around, and white sails tall and billowing, and it was never a modern ship, because the words came from long ago somewhere, coming like the ship against the grey distance, like from China or Australia.

Our noses ran. In summer, it could be from pollen, or from the dust of cornfields, or from playing in bracken on the warren. In winter, it was the cold weather, or 'catching a cold'.

You might feel a drip running down to your top lip and trying to get into your mouth, even if it had to run into the corner first. You might try to catch it on your sleeve or the back of your hand, if there was no time to reach for your 'hanky'. If you did have time, you had to hope the hanky wasn't getting too wet — wet to your fingers, wet to your nose, and sometimes wet to your leg when it was back in your trouser-pocket. Sometimes, you didn't have a hanky anyway. It was still where your mother had put it, ready to pick up. Some mothers might not have put it there on that day, or, some, on any day.

Some children often had 'candles' running down from their snouts. Almost always, it was the same boys. Mrs Hart would tell someone sharply, 'Wipe your nose.' Then she might say, 'No, not the back of your hand!' And she might get an old square of rag from somewhere, and hold it out.

'Use that, and put it in your pocket. And everyone, *ev-er-ry-one*, have a *handkerchief* in your pocket or up your sleeve tomorrow'.

Older boys said 'snot' and 'snot-rags'. At birthdays and Christmas, people who didn't bother to spend much time looking-for, or making, good presents, would give handkerchiefs. There must have been drawers full of them all over England. Some people passed them on to someone else at the next birthday or Christmas.

Some men had a 'nasty habit', as Mum said, when they were walking along or riding a bike, of just holding their nose between thumb and finger then blowing and flicking their snot away. You had to 'watch out' if you were close behind, because they didn't think of looking round, or didn't care.

You might think, well, at least someone won't have to wash his hanky.

Ruth Rudd was a girl in the little school. She had a nice-sounding name, and it suited her because she had a beautiful face, with eyes that looked as if she liked all she could see. But her seeing it was cut short, because she died, and we were sad for a long time because it seemed unfair that it should happen, whatever people might say about 'God's Will', and all the things that get said. Ruth died of 'tb', which some people called consumption or 'the consumption'. She was delicate, and beautiful, and good to remember, although it always made you a bit frightened at the same time.

Dad made a hoop of iron, welded it to join the rod into a perfect ring. It bowled along the Council Road as fast as I could run, and faster, with a little rod I held hooked on the near-side, halfway between the mid-point and the speeding ground. It was a beauty, better than all the other hoops around. The 'usual' were rims of bike wheels with the spokes knocked out. You bowled them with a stick, and careful whacks. Too light, and they would wobble, turn, and fall; too hard, and they might skid. The best way was to hold the stick straight down, inside the rim-grove, where the tube and tyre had been, and push it as you ran. It 'took some doing', but it worked awhile. It all came to an end with 'growing out of it', and when, around that time, the hoop my dad had made rolled into Rod Alley pit and sank where the water went down deep.

We started watching out for number plates on cars. There were always letters before the numbers. The letters we liked spotting most were NBG, and we called out 'No Bloody Good', and we laughed again, as if it was still a good joke long after we were tired of it.

❧

This wind, this wind that makes the whole house shake, not really, but that's how it seems.

Things outside bang-bang about, turning over, rolling, falling, sliding, tumble, crash, scrape, whistle, creak, crack, slam, and whine: little live things crouching under somewhere, somewhere, staying still, some bolt, or scuttle, burrow, cling together, try not to fall, and listen for some other sound than this, this, this, this going on all night, until, until ...

CHAPTER 9

A horse and rider, early every Sunday evening, cantered across the Green. They came from the Chattergate corner, broke into a canter immediately, and slowed down at the road to Banham, about midway of the Green's far side. The rider was Mr Oliver, a farmer from about two miles up Abbey Road. He always wore a broad-brimmed Stetson hat, which made him seem like someone from the Wild West. He was on his way to evening service at Banham Church. It seemed likely that he so much enjoyed his canter across the Green that this was the main reason we saw him. The horse enjoyed it too. It was easy to imagine that a look in its eyes always told his master yes if he seemed to be asking, 'Shall we go this week?' Mr Oliver was not seen much in the village. There was interest in what was said about his romance with Miss Simpson, daughter of another farmer. The Simpsons were a posh family. Part of the road to Attleborough was called Simpson's Hill. Mr Oliver was called a 'gentleman farmer', which meant that he owned the farm but had several men to do the hard work. Most of the farmers had to do most of the work themselves. Some didn't own their farms. They were called 'tenant farmers'.

I always loved seeing horse and rider from the window by my grandfather's desk. The horse's legs always looked forward and back, as in the old-fashioned pictures.

On the white marble mantelpiece in the drawing room at Sunnyside, there was a large French clock, golden, with a round white face and black Roman numbers. Grandad lifted off the tall glass cover with the dome-shaped top, and put it gently on the table. He gave a few careful turns of the winding key, and stood back, listening, looking pleased, before he put the cover over, and the ticks were gone.

Mr Elvin sailed round the Post Office corner on his bike from the road alongside the old foundry and the blacksmith's shop. I was on my bike on the little road in front of the Rod Alley pit. It was certain that he would crash into me or pitch into the water. Instead, he tried to make his turn sharper. There was a look of fright on his face. His bike reared up, so he landed among his 'Clean Easy' wares from the carrier over the front wheel.

He stood up, shouting, and pointing at his buckled wheel.

'Look at that. Look at that. Who's goin' t' put that right? I know. Old Cuckoo! Old Cuckoo can put it right. We'll go and see Old Cuckoo.'

Old Cuckoo was my grandfather. In his schooldays he was given the nickname because he mispronounced 'cocoa' in a reading aloud lesson. It stayed with him all his childhood, and in adult life was brought out by anyone who had reason for using it behind his back. Mr Elvin would never have thought of calling him Cuckoo to his face any more than Grandad would have called him Pippin. The name Pippin Elvin seemed to say something about the man, but we didn't know what. He had very shiny brown shoes. He had a different sort of job from other men of the village, and dressed differently from most of them.

When he was ready to set off for Sunnyside, Mr Elvin was still talking partly to himself, partly to anyone who might hear. He had difficulty in wheeling the bike, stopping often as he pushed along the narrow path made by my grandfather's daily walking. He took to lifting the front wheel off the ground altogether. I had little memory of what was said when we got to Sunnyside. Grandad must have agreed to give the money for a new wheel. We stood outside the back door. I shut myself off from what was said because I was being made to feel entirely to blame for the accident. Grandad did not ask me about it afterwards.

We travelled to London on a yellow and red lorry of Mid-Norfolk Dairies, Dad and me sitting with the driver. It was a very early morning start, and the first hour was taken up by the many stops that had to be made for the collection of full churns set out in yards or gateways. Then the driver started to pick up speed, and the stops were fewer. Passing through small towns, where most of the shops and people clustered alongside the main road, was the beginning of an adventure that was free because Dad's cousin Ada was married to the Mid-Norfolk Dairies manager. His name was Reg Hart, and he was our headmaster's brother, but a very different kind of man.

When we reached London, Uncle Oliver, was waiting for us. He was tall and strong-looking, in a smart grey suit. It didn't seem odd that he had the same name as a farmer back in Old Buckenham, but it was surprising that my uncle must also once have been a horseman. He had been in the 'Mounties' in Canada, which made me proud that he was my uncle. Now he took us to his home in Southall, and his family of Aunt Ethel and the two boys, Herbert and Charles. Charles was always called Chum. He was four months younger than me, but Herbert was about five years older, and more apart. One of the first things to notice was that Londoners seemed cleverer and more assured than we were. The way they spoke was posher. It was easy to believe that London schools were better than any in Norfolk. Chum always looked very sure in things he said. He had a round, often-smiling, slightly freckly face.

We were in London for the Silver Jubilee celebrations for King George the Fifth and Queen Mary. It was 1935, so Dad was thirty-five years old, and I was nine. Next day, we were part of the crowd in Trafalgar Square, waiting for the royal procession. I was overwhelmed by the noise and crowding, and spent some time sitting on someone's leather case on the paving, with only a small gap of sky beyond their shoulders. The crowd started to cheer. I was unexpectedly up on one of the famous sculpture lions and the procession was passing somewhere among the throng.

Next day, we went home on the milk lorry. Before we left, Chum asked me something.

'Do you know why Mother is not going to invite you to stay again?'

'No.'

'You piss the bed.'

When little Kathleen Whitehand reached the age of fourteen, she had to leave school, as was usual in those days for children at all 'Elementary' council schools. She was sent to London to work for a wealthy lady in a house in South Kensington, a Mrs Van der Something. Kathleen liked her and was happy there. Her work was doing all the jobs a domestic servant would learn to do, and she stayed there until she was twenty, when she married my father, and came back to Old Buckenham.

A very surprising thing about her was that, although she had not gone on beyond thirteen years of age at school, she knew a great many poems by heart. She told me many of them, and I always enjoyed hearing them. She knew them so very well that she never had to read them to me. She didn't ever have poems in books anyway. They were in her head, and how they got there, I didn't know. She recalled them without any struggle. Many of their lines stayed in my head too, but I would never have thought of knowing every one. To her it seemed an ordinary thing, but she must have known it was not ordinary. All were poems that told good stories, all of long ago.

My mother talked about her childhood sometimes, not very much because her mother died when she was twelve. Her sister Mabel was fourteen. Mabel had lived away a while, with Aunt Allie in 'The Star' at Diss. After her mother died, she came home, 'kept house' for her father, cared for the family. Percy was a little older, Willie, older still. Younger than my mother, were Dick and Maudie.

She had a tiny room in Mrs Van der Something's house, up near the roof, to be herself in when the work was done, the washing-up, the dusting, dusting, dusting, shining, shining, scouring, peeling, chipping, chopping, washing, washing, rinsing, rinsing, doing what you're told, all that and more, 'Yes, Mrs Van der Something', 'No, Mrs Van der Something', and lie here, thinking: Old Buckenham, Stacksford, Willie, Percy, Mabel, little Maudie, Dick, the field behind, the sunset over it, the old privy with three holes and lids (parent, in-between, and small), quite a bit different from South Kensington, got to black-lead the kitchen range tomorrow, hate that job, oh, go to sleep, the heather on the warren, the little stream at the meadow bottom, slowly, slowly, a little ripple keeps coming, a little sparkle, slowly on ... 'It was a summer evening, Old Kaspar's work was done, And he before his cottage door, Was sitting in the sun, And by him sported on the green His little grandchild, Wilhelmine...'

'You might as well give an old sow a strawberry,' Mum said. It was when someone was mean in giving something, especially something to eat. You imagined a very big old sow putting her great snout down to a little strawberry, and snorting.

'My dad could fight your dad.' When you said it you knew you were trying to make someone think it was true. You thought it was true yourself. But he said his dad could fight yours, and he thought that was true. When we said 'fight', it meant 'fight and beat'. Our dads could have been proud of what we said, but they never knew we said it

Each path across the Green was straight. The older ones were deeper worn, their dark earth bare from boots and shoes of centuries, fringes of grass kept short by people sometimes walking wider side by side. Paths went to church. They went to school. Some crossed or joined another, turned off to shops, or corners, for the roads that went to somewhere else.. It made you think how many walked each day, and why, and all the years. But mostly, it was good to play in that long grass awhile and be away from ways to anywhere. The cows came close to look at you, with wondering eyes. Sometimes we held a buttercup under each other's chins to see if it made a reflection on the skin.. Some skins reflected better than others. A girl you liked looked even prettier with the yellow light touching there But we were usually only boys together, and it was strange and exciting on anyone We made it seem more ordinary by saying 'See if you like butter' as the reason for doing it, because a good reflection was supposed to show that you did. We were always disappointed if there wasn't a good result, and we knew it didn't really show anything about butter at all.

People on the Green went on Shanks's pony, Mum said. Somebody said it was the biggest village Green in Norfolk. Somebody else said it was the biggest in England.

To mark the Silver Jubilee of King George V, an oak tree was planted on the far side of the Council Road, opposite the Green end of Rod Alley. Round it was built a beautiful wooden seat, really four seats joined at the corners, with a good space in the middle for the tree to grow big over the centuries. The seat was made of Japanese oak, which I had never heard of till then, but the tree was an English oak. It was the kind of celebration of the Jubilee that made people proud, because it was better than things done in most other villages, and it would be remembered for all the centuries the tree lasted.

An event that was very special to me happened soon after.

The spinney pond was still, partly shadowed by trees and bushes. I had never seen it so early. Uncle Oliver, who was staying with my grandparents for a short holiday, called to collect me and we came the two miles on our bikes.

We baited hooks and cast, and sat silent. Uncle Oliver had his pipe. He was not silent all the while. He talked intelligently, not wasting words. He would not say anything so cleverly that it might worry me. But he would not say things that did not need answering. Occasionally, either of us might see his float dipping or being tugged across the surface. Sometimes, with a red flash of fins and tail, a roach was swinging clear of the water, to our murmurs of excitement and applause. Sometimes it was the rarer, dark backed thrill of a tench. Uncle Oliver's unspoken rule was that everything we took out would be put back, even if there was a delay for gloating over a frantically circling guest in a jar.

It was good to be there with Uncle Oliver. Everything about it was good. I took the hook out of a fish's mouth carefully so as to do no damage, and felt good when the fish darted off to safety. Dragonflies skimmed over the bright water, and this was a perfect place to be.

CHAPTER 10

We called him 'Little Wilfy'. He was nine, small for his age, and timid. He was glad to be in one of my grandfather's living vans on the Green, no longer in a tent. He had been travelling with his grandfather and grandmother, whose only home was the tiny tent.

I had read the little book, *Gypsy Dick* , over and over, imagining myself as Dick. I had long outgrown the easy words, but stayed with Dick because I loved the story. I said to Little Wilfy that it must be good to move on each day, not to be in one place always. He said it was not good to keep on moving. It was not good to live in a tiny tent. It was good to be here in a living van. He had a new suit, which he wore for school only. We knew he must be scared of school, because he was not used to it. But he was so pleased to be here now, and he wanted to stay.

One day we crept under the living van to hear him getting a hiding from his grandmother.

'You little sod,' she kept saying. Her voice was breathless, with the energy she used, 'You … little … sod!'

We heard the leather hitting him, his cries. We ran away before the door opened and the old woman looked out. Her head had a shiny growth among the hair, like a reddish plum.

There was a pile of brown cotton cloth on the big table of the drawing room at Sunnyside, and Aunt Ethel was busy at Grandma's sewing machine. What caught my eye was a length of decoration in green similar to the decoration down the trouser seams and round the tunic edges of my cousin Chum's Red Indian outfit. I stood watching.

'What are you making?'

'Some Indian curtains.'

There seemed something wrong with the answer, but she was busy and needed to say no more before I went out. My birthday was a few days later. There was never a gift as perfect as my Indian suit. Seeing Chum in his outfit made me see how he could put on the clothes and not be changed by them into someone no longer just himself.

One day we were in the orchard, where Aunt Violet's chickens moved about freely much of the time. They had a 'run' surrounded by wire netting at the top end of the orchard, with shelter, and boxes for nesting, where they were kept in sometimes behind a wire netting gate with a wooden frame. Chum seized a hen that was not in the run, held it by its legs, and flung it, squawking, over the high netting. We had not noticed that the gate was not quite closed. In a moment, the hen was out through the gap and pecking wildly at Chum's legs. As he shouted and kicked, it turned aside, now pecking at my knees, frantically squawking.

We ran down the orchard with the chicken following. At the iron fencing, we scrambled through on to the driveway, not far from the back door of the house. The hen followed through, still as wild as before. Desperate, I seized it by the neck, pressed its head to the gravel, and, with terror, stamped on it as hard as I could, feeling bones crunch. There's no more memory. I have a vague feeling that we took the creature and put it in the run, saying nothing to anyone. We never spoke of it again. I have wondered if the killing really happened. Aunt Violet never mentioned losing a chicken.

Over the garden railings of Uncle Leslie's house, Aunt Ethel, who was on one of her short stays at Sunnyside, was talking to Leslie's wife, Ruth. As I passed on my way home, they noticed me and said my name in greeting. As I got to our gate, I knew that Aunt Ethel said something about me. It was something like, 'His sisters are made too much of ... He has to fit in to suit them ... Not fair on him ...' It seemed that Aunt Ethel could have sympathy with a boy because she had only boys. I didn't hear what Aunt Ruth said. She had four girls. What Aunt Ethel said was good to hear, but I wasn't sure that it was true. Perhaps it was on this holiday that she told my mother that she didn't really like being at Sunnyside because some of the other aunts, Grandma's grown up children, didn't make her feel at ease whenever they came on visits. They treated her as if she was 'not good enough for them'. She meant two aunts in particular, Ruth (another one) and Elsie.

Aunts Ruth and Elsie were great friends, and they always made their visits home to Sunnyside at the same time, coming from different directions, Ruth from Wisbech, in Cambridgeshire, Elsie from Lowestoft, in Suffolk. One year, for my Christmas presents, they each kitted a jersey. Aunt Ruth's was in a mixture of reddish shades, with bright red 'bobbles' standing out all over, like no other jersey I had ever seen. Aunt Elsie's was more ordinary, in light brown, with tiny whitish flecks. I loved to be in both, but much preferred the red. It was easy to realize that each present showed something about the person who chose the wool and imagined what it would look like on me. Aunt Ruth was jolly, and laughed a lot. She seemed a bold sort of lady, and liked acting in plays. Aunt Elsie was more serious, sometimes grumpy, and not as good-looking as her sister.

> Tinker, tailor, soldier, sailor,
> Rich man, poor man,
> Beggar man, thief.
> This year, next year,
> Some time, never.

Every year, when plums were ripe, we often had plums and custard. So, time after time, never tiring of it, we said the old rhymes, to learn what we would become. As the words seemed only to be for boys, my sisters could use the plum stones to see which kind of man they might marry.

Almost always, each day's stones gave us different answers, but we still liked to feel that it was not silly to want to find what they foretold. Sometimes, even on the same day, if we had a second helping the extra plums could give a different forecast. Mum always took a great interest and amusement in seeing what was ahead for us in our lives, and if the story in the stones was not what we wanted she could say it might not come true. Tomorrow was 'another day'. We didn't get down from the table without that game.

With 'This year, next year ...' we could choose for ourselves what would or wouldn't happen. It could be something we wanted or didn't want. We kept it secret. The plates were always scraped clean. The stones round the rim were clean too.

Fly-papers were in every house. A usual place to hang one was above a table, so people wouldn't collide with it. When bought, they were in neat little rolls, with a string at one end so they could be pinned to a ceiling or tied to something overhead before being pulled out. As soon as one was hanging, a fly would settle, perhaps licking at the brown sticky stuff, and try to walk. But there was no walking on a fly-paper, and no more walking, ever, for that fly. It might try to tug its legs away, but they would stay stuck. Wings would flap as the fly twisted and turned, and they, too, might stick. We didn't watch it much, because we were so used to it. Perhaps we sometimes hoped a certain fly would get away and have the sense to get out of the house. But it didn't get away. I never saw one go. They all were soon no more than dead flies, above our heads, as we ate the food they could have been on if they'd had the sense to wait.

Under most people's beds there were chamber-pots. They usually had flowers painted on the white background. Ours had red roses and their leaves. The pots were usually quite heavy so they wouldn't tip over if anyone was careless. The one Dad used might start the night under the bed, but in the morning it would be about four feet away, towards the window. It was on the left side of the bed, and on his own left side as he got out, which must have been more than once in the night, even though he went to bed late and got up early. By getting-up time it was always full.

Soon after breakfast, and after 'time for school', Mum would be carefully on her way down the stairs with her blue-enamelled slop-pail with a lid that stopped the load from spilling as she moved. In the bedroom, the 'chamber' would be gleaming after the rinse with hot water. There would be only a very few days in the year on which the pail did not have its journey up and down the steep stairs and out into the yard. Mum had her own chamber on her side. You wouldn't know it was there if you hadn't used it yourself, when you came into the big bed when you were younger.

Some people called a chamber pot a 'Jerry' or 'Jerry-pot', Some said 'piss-pot'.

Mr Nice, was a policeman at New Buckenham when I was nine or ten, perhaps earlier or later too. It seemed odd that a man who had to catch people out for doing wrong should be called Nice. We, somehow, expected him to be nasty.

I sang 'Red Sails in the Sunset'.

> Red sails in the sunset
> Way out on the sea,
> Oh, carry my loved one
> Home safely to me.
>
> He sailed at the dawning,
> All day I've been blue,
> Red sails in the sunset
> I'm trusting in you.

It made a picture in my thoughts like the one in the girl's eyes, shadows of evening everywhere except on a patch of the sea, where the gold-red sun, from the land behind, was touching across the water, catching the sails of a fishing-boat that was still far off, but coming in, trying to reach land before darkness came down. I was watching, and wanting the wind to bring the boat in safely. Lots of people sang this song: all those little fishing-boats coming to shore in the near-darkness, even in the brightness of morning, wherever we happened to be, George Jolly on his bread cart, Uncle Dick trotting Dinah, someone on their bike, anyone, anywhere.

I knew who Hauptmann was. It was said he kidnapped and murdered 'the Lindbergh baby'.

He was going to be executed. There had been pages about the crime in the newspapers three years earlier. The baby's father was Charles Lindbergh, the famous airman, who had been the first man to fly across the Atlantic. I possibly heard about it then, the flying and the kidnapping, but perhaps I didn't, because I was only five at the time of the kidnapping in 1932, and the famous flight had been several years before that. I knew who Hauptmann was because Uncle Oliver and some of my aunts were talking about him at Sunnyside. One thing I'm not sure of is what Uncle Oliver was saying about Hauptmann. I started listening when I heard him say the name. But I had not noticed the first part of what he said. It was too late to begin listening, but I did. Children were not supposed to ask questions about adult conversations. Uncle Oliver would have been pleased to hear one, but everybody else would have believed 'children should be seen, not heard'. So I have never been sure about what he thought about Hauptmann being guilty or innocent. I thought he was innocent. I would have liked Uncle Oliver to agree. I think he did.

Whenever there was a murder written about in the newspapers, people talked about it. They liked to argue about who did it. When someone was caught and accused, they liked to discuss whether he was guilty. They mostly seemed to say he was. There was one murder that was still talked about even though it had happened in 1910. It was said that Dr Crippen had murdered his wife and fled to Canada with another woman. The story was still told because it was the first time the new invention of wireless had been used to catch a criminal. A message was sent from the ship, back to London, saying that Dr Crippen was on board. A detective took a faster ship and was waiting to make an arrest when Crippen arrived. He was hanged all those years ago, but was still talked about.

Little Wilfy sat on the grass near the living van, blowing a mouth-organ. He couldn't play it properly, but only made a bit of a tune to please himself as he sat there alone. When I came up he didn't know whether to stop, and would have stopped because he was showing he couldn't play it properly, but he saw that I didn't think it too bad, so carried on, suck and blow, suck and blow, pretending it was real playing, like any of us did. I said it was a nice mouth-organ. He said yes it was, then, 'It was yours. Your mother gave it to me.'

I didn't say he should give it back, because it was not his fault that she had given it. She was always doing things like that, being generous, with good feelings like wanting a boy like Wilfy to have a mouth-organ, even if it left me without one.

One day, before long, Wilfy had gone. His grandfather and grandmother decided to go back to their tent, and we never heard of little Wilfy again. I remembered him saying, no, it was not good to keep on moving, and thought of the day we sat under the living van while the old woman was giving him the strap, shouting, 'You … little … sod'.

CHAPTER 11

Home from hospital, with my tonsils taken out, I became ill. This was a surprise, because Doctor Bruce had said the operation would be good for me. Days passed, more days, and more.

I was in the back bedroom, next to my parents' bedroom. It overlooked the garden and the orchard, but I didn't want to look out. Uncle Willie, Mum's oldest brother, who had been ill after a bad car accident, and had just come back from a cruise around Africa, which was to make him feel better, came to show off his monkey. It was on a leather lead, like a little dog. It jumped about the bedclothes and was full of curiosity about everything it could touch. But it was no help at making me better. Doctor Bruce came often, and one day he brought a Stanley Gibbons stamp catalogue, which belonged to his wife. It showed all the world's stamps. But it made me no better.

Then, one day when I slid out of bed, I went to the window. Perhaps I was already feeling a bit better, because what I saw outside made me eager to get out. Under the trees of the orchard, the cow parsley had grown tall and burst into flower, so it looked a wonderland of whiteness gleaming under the branches, which were just opening their own buds of leaves and blossom. Before many days had passed, I was parting stalks as I made my stealthy way among the flowers, pausing, from moment to moment, to sit in delight at being there.

Robinson Crusoe was the book my mother chose when I might understand if she read carefully, leaving out the hard bits, hard to her as well as me. She very much enjoyed the reading, pausing, reading from a short way on. Even if she read the hard bits, it made sense enough to keep me listening. And so I heard a book so strong in holding me that it would be, for always, part of what I know. I went back to it later when I could read it for myself, but perhaps it never was so good as when I found myself alone upon a shore Mum showed me, with the sea, the wreck, the things we fetched from it, the days and days when we were castaways.

Everyone had something wrong with them. Before I went to have my tonsils out, I had to go to be examined at the Norfolk and Norwich Hospital. Mum sat with me in the waiting room. There were many people. We had to sit in rows while people took their turn at going forward to be examined by a doctor who was sitting where we could see him as he worked. While we were waiting, I saw something that really scared me. A lady was having her eyes, or an eye, looked at. The doctor picked up a syringe to give her an injection somewhere near an eye, and suddenly blood was running down her face. Mum saw it too and she must have been as scared as I was. I think a nurse wiped the blood away, and when the lady went, another nurse came for me. Mum couldn't come. She had to sit and wait for me. I think she must have said, 'You'll be all right. He'll just look down your throat'. He did. I felt 'real scared', was shivering. He put a wood thing in, to press my tongue down. I think he said, 'Say "Aarh', like doctors do. I think he pinched my nose. I stood up to go back to Mum. All those faces looked at me. She wasn't there. Someone said, 'She'll be all right. She just went a little faint.' They took me to another room, where Mum was sat. She said that she was sorry but she'd fainted. We went home on the red 'United' bus. 'Well, that was a funny old day,' I suppose she said.

A book about Lawrence of Arabia was what I chose on the day I went into hospital. Aunt

Violet came with Mum. We went to Jarrold's bookshop first, so they could buy me a book to read in hospital and afterwards. We went round shelves so I could choose. I found a fairly thick one on Lawrence of Arabia. They looked at it. They said it was 'a bit too old'. I knew they meant too difficult to read. I really wanted it, but hadn't thought about the price. There were two more, both thinner. One was about geography, *British North Borneo*. I loved geography with Mrs Hart. The other was a 'Rupert' book, bright yellow covered. I had to make my mind up. Then Aunt Violet said, 'Have both'. We went a children's hospital called the Jenny Lind.

Next day we had to sit in a circle. At first, it was like a game. They gave us all a rubber bathing cap that covered tight, with a strap around your chin. They were different colours. I didn't remember which I had. When we had got them on, we did interesting things. I can't remember what they were. I think we listened to a gramophone, and said some rhymes, but I'm not sure. There was a trolley that we had to be put on, one by one. They didn't come back, but the trolley did, then someone else was lifted on and went away. When my turn came, I wanted to be helpful because of feeling scared and I was older than the rest because I was nine, so I tried to get on the trolley by myself instead of waiting to be lifted up, but couldn't manage it, and got told off for trying anyway, and the angry woman lifted me and I went off and can't remember any more until I was waking up with everybody crying in the ward.

'I want my mum,' they kept on crying. I kept quiet because of being older, listening to them. 'I want my mum, my mum, my mum.' Then one voice somewhere said, 'I want my dad.'

Next day, someone said that, in the night, two boys had tried to get out of a window and climb down a drainpipe to the ground. I didn't know if it was true.

Dad and Mum came to take me home in the car. Halfway home, I was very thirsty, so Dad drove into the yard of a very old farmhouse and asked if I could have a drink of milk. I had a mug of milk straight from a churn. And soon we were on our way. When I woke the following morning I was very ill with a fever.

Dad said the cause was likely to be the milk I had been given. Doctor Bruce said it was more likely to be the surgical instruments at the hospital not being sterilized properly. But whatever the cause, it was the worst illness I had ever had, and that was why I had my visit from Uncle Willie's monkey. Uncle Willie himself never got well again, and did not live long. The little monkey must have pined for him.

The spare front bedroom overlooked the pit, with the morning light across fields, the

Green, and water. I went in from my little room next to it, with a small window that faced to the orchard and sunsets. One day I opened some of the full drawers in the big chest and happened upon a dress of patterned green and was fascinated by its strangeness. It was from long ago in my mother's life, and she was happy to let me play with it. I took it outside, and in the foundry yard, in the grassy place where I had put my tent, I tried it on. The play in my head was to imagine what it was like to be a girl, what it might be like to be a redskin girl. I stayed in the tent for a long time, with the light coming through the canvas, in a dream of different ways of being someone I was not, a brown-skinned girl in a green garment that had the power to make that difference and take me away with it. I wanted nothing else, but to be content in where I was and what I was feeling. Later, the dress could go back in its place, and I never thought to look at it again.

The workshops were silent and full of shadows when the men were away in the fields. I walked in almost as if trespassing. Footsteps were quiet because the floor was the earth. There were no boards, only the earth as it had been worn by all the feet going over it, dipping in places where some of the jobs were done. Like where the big vices held iron in their grip by the window benches along the front, or where bellows were worked, in a dark recess at the side of the furnace where the coals were stored, or round the anvil, or the corn scales. Or by the long lathe under the window on 'Uncle Harry's side', though this lathe came later than most of the other things, and its long treadle took much of the weight of boots. Look back from the window, and you see the little engine that would start immediately to life at the pull of a lever to drive anything for which power was needed.

The corn scales were in a corner near the sliding doors at the front of the workshop, just before the yard between Grandad's place and Uncle Harry's. The part the sacks of corn were put in to be weighed looked like the back half of a rounded cage. It was made of iron: the half circle of floor, some upright bars, more bars crossing around them to make the rounded back and sides. It was a little wider than a soldier's sentry box, and almost as high. A large sack of corn could stand in there. The weights would balance on the right hand side, put on an iron platform suspended on a rod down to its centre, the top linked to a balancing bar the cage was hung from too.

I tried to weigh myself, but didn't manage it. You needed to stand in the cage, have someone else to put the weights on, one by one. But I was on my own. I think Dad helped me once, but that was too early to remember. I could have been imagining, 'All in your imagination,' Mum might say. The point is, when the corn was weighed, the weights were put on till the two sides balanced, both just off the ground. You would count the total of the weights. You might have added as you put them on.

The big weights were square-sided, solid iron, with a moulded handle at the top, the figures cast into the top as well. Even the small ones were the same, but there were small round weights too. Another way to measure wheat, oats and barley was in a bushel skep, which was rounded like a barrel, made of strong light wood. One always stood beside the scales

Come back to thinking about the worn earth floor, the silence and shadows. The front of the workshops has another room, small, beyond the stairway, not much used. Also not much used now is the great foundry room, filling all the back of the building. There are many things to show what went on in the days when it gave the whole building its name. I never saw it in those days. There are still many things that were cast here. They lie about, unwanted, among the other abandoned things, tongs, wooden shapes from which casts were taken. In a corner, a passage leads to a little room that contains one car, an old Peugeot, stripped down to its working parts, facing a door to the yard, from where it is used to drive something, with its power turning through a flapping belt, to drive anything that needs driving, a saw-bench, a threshing drum.

After the darkness of the workshop, it was always good to be in the sunshine between the old trees of the orchard. 'An apple a day keeps the doctor away,' Mum said. I knew it wasn't quite true. Sometimes in summer I ate apples straight off the trees till I got the bellyache.

CHAPTER 12

The great horse is a stallion. We wait to see if he will kick.

'Stand up,' shouts Tip. His cap and red face are grubby from his work.

He takes the left hind hock between his knees, his leather apron opening. He pulls the old shoe off, and drops it. He picks up a blade to smooth the hoof. Quick slices fall. He takes a shoe old Edgar's made and brings on tongs. Hoof sizzles, smokes. We breathe the stink, the lovely stink of it. Tip grumbles as he works. Sometimes it's to himself, sometimes the horse, or us. He does not swear. Old Edgar is a chapel man. Tip takes the hooves in turn. Each time he moves, we watch for trouble, but the horse stands calm. Old Edgar, smiling, comes and goes from the smoky place where he tends the furnace and hammers red-hot iron on the anvil. There is a stall where men can pee while waiting for their horse. They do not use it while we're here. The stallion lets a fart and turns his head, and nods as if he's pleased. Tip says something. The men laugh.

It's 1935. There is a war in Abyssinia. In the *Express* a black man lay, with frightened eyes, and one arm raised to shield his head, from the rifle-butt of an Italian.

People who only knew Tip Self in his daytime job would not have recognized him on summer evenings. As soon as he had eaten a quick meal, he was starting up his motorbike and edging bike and sidecar through his gateway. Scrubbed and white-coated, he was an ice cream man, off on his rounds, most of his customers knowing nothing of how he spent his days. His wife made the ice cream at their house, which was at the side of the road on the way from New Buckenham, and Tip had no difficulty in selling it. There were always customers ready to rush out to buy, glad to have Tip instead of a man called Fiddler Wright, who had a habit of spitting on his hands and rubbing them together before taking up cones and wafers and digging his spatula into the can. I am not sure I ever saw him do that, but the story was the usual thing to be told of him.

'A lot of squit and nonsense,' Mum said. Both words seemed to mean the same thing. But sometimes they were separate. 'That's squit', or 'That's nonsense'. And it usually was.

When Aunt Hilda came 'home' to Sunnyside for a few days, her husband, Uncle Jack, came too. Like her, he was posh, speaking in a 'la-di-dah' voice. He was very tall and he wore 'plus fours', which looked like very baggy trousers but ended just below his knees, with thick socks pulled up to them. The only other man in the village who wore plus fours was Spike Loveday, one of our relatives whose connection was never clear except in his name. He was a bit of a show-off, especially with his harmonica, which he could play very well. But his plus fours never made him posh like Uncle Jack, who was simply posh by nature. He was so posh that he never stayed at Sunnyside when he came, but at the end of each day would drive off alone to the Royal Hotel in Attleborough for the night, coming back after breakfast. Perhaps this was because there was no separate bed for him at Sunnyside because other aunts and uncles came to visit at the same time. Why he didn't sleep with Aunt Hilda, we never knew. I always thought it was because he loved the Royal Hotel, until it occurred to me that he probably didn't sleep with Aunt Hilda in their house either.

Of the ten children born to Grandma, four were girls. Only Aunt Hilda was married. Mum said aunts Violet, Ruth, and Elsie were 'maiden aunts' or 'spinsters'. They all seemed to like posh Uncle Jack. Aunt Hilda was their elder sister. She smoked her cigarettes in a long cigarette holder. She had brrn to universty and was very clever, and she knew it. She had golden hair, straight, and cut short round her neck.

Grandad and his brother Arthur had quarrelled over something even my mother didn't talk about. It could have be. en that she didn't know the reason for the quarrel. She said it was started by their wives. I never thought about it much. We never had anything to do with that side of the family at all. Dad never mentioned it or his Uncle Arthur, who was another threshing man. The brothers' machines must have done most of the threshing for many miles around.

For their parents' Golden Wedding anniversary in 1935, some of their children suggested there should be a 'making up' and invitations sent. Grandad or Grandma, or both, would not agree.

There was a gathering of all their children and their families, except for Charles, dead in the Great War, and Philip, probably dead in Canada or the USA. It was a sunny day. We were mostly on the lawn. I was nine. There was a photograph.

Behind Sunnyside, under the two great walnut trees in the orchard, there was a very old machine I called 'the motorbike', but it was really a motor-tricycle. There were two wheels in front of the handlebars, and, in between them, there had once been a wicker-basket seat, in which Grandma had sat, with Grandad taking her for a ride when he was a proud young man. Nowadays, she was always dressed in black or other dark clothes, but I imagined her in long, pretty, wide skirts, like the ladies in picture-books. And it seemed, oh so far off and long ago, long, long before the Great War came.

A car came down the Green, a large one, steadily, almost slow. It passed Rod Alley. Because it was large, and very high, it almost looked like an empty car, finding its own way. Then you saw the solitary man, upright, in dark jacket and bowler hat, in all that emptiness, sitting tight, looking only straight ahead.

'That's Uncle Arthur,' my mother said.

CHAPTER 13

I watched someone making 'ducks and drakes', then tried it myself. You had to make a stone skim over the water, just touching the surface, and bouncing up, touching, bouncing, touching, bouncing, as far as it would go. The flatter the stone, the better it worked. A small piece of slate was best. When you tried, everyone was watching. They watched while you could do it. When you couldn't, they soon turned away.

Francis Loveday was not my cousin, but he was some sort of relative. He was never called Francis except by 'old lady Lovedi', his grandmother, who looked after him. We all called him 'Stoot', which was our way of saying 'stoat'. It didn't sound a name anybody would have liked to have, but he was used to it. The old lady called him from her gate at Sunnyside

Cottages, a small row backing on to the meadow with the tennis court at Sunnyside. She made the 'Fran' part rhyme with 'man'. We made it rhyme with 'barn'.

One day, 'Stoot' stood close to the water of the Rod Alley pit, at the place where there was a dip of several steps, just opposite our front gate. He had a long piece of leafy willow, which he let over his head to the water behind him then swished up to splash us. We squealed and stepped aside, and he tried again, getting more excited and determined as we kept shifting away and coming back. Suddenly, he lost his balance and fell over backwards into the water. He struggled to his feet, soaked. As he went off, we laughed behind him.

Spike Loveday, the son of 'old lady Lovedi', played his harmonica and sang. We loved his 'Buddy, can you spare a dime?' at concerts in the village hall. He gave us that one every time.

We had a gramophone, but not a good one. You had to wind it up by a little crank on the side. We had hardly any records to play, and they were old and sounded scratchy, or the needle got stuck in a groove and played the same line over and over, so we did not 'try it again' very often.

Mum said her favourite singer was Count John McCormack. Perhaps that was because one of his songs was 'I'll take you home again, Kathleen' and she could pretend it was being sung to her especially. We didn't have a radio till I was eleven, so she couldn't hear her song much anywhere. One of the records we had, and seemed to play every time the gramophone came out, was Harry Lauder singing 'Keep right on to the end of the road'. We went to see him when he came to a theatre in Norwich. But that was too early in my life for me to remember clearly. I liked the song, even though it was about being old and struggling on. Each generation of our family was able to say they saw some famous theatre person. Grandad saw Sir Henry Irving. My parents saw Harry Lauder. I shall mention someone later.

'Two Little Girls in Blue' was one of Dad's favourite songs. I didn't know it was old when I first heard it.

Two little girls in blue, lad,
Two little girls in blue.
They were sisters, we were brothers,
And we learned to love the two.

One little girl in blue, lad,
She won your father's heart.
She became your mother, I married the other,
But now we have drifted apart.

When Dad sang it, I had the feeling that he liked it so much that it must be about his own life. I didn't try to think clearly. It was like dreaming. I wondered who the girls were. They didn't seem just girls in a song. One of them seemed like my mother when she was very young and beautiful, like someone who would win somebody's heart. Even when I thought of it as just a favourite song, there was still a sense of it being something more.

My teacher in the big school was Miss Holmes. She was pretty, and wore pretty dresses, and under them was the loveliest bosom anyone could imagine. But after a short while, she became Mrs Lincoln, by marrying a farmer who lived somewhere beyond Attleborough. He was a very tall man, people said, called 'Long Lincoln'. I never saw him but just imagined him. Everybody at school liked Mrs Lincoln, and I was sorry she had married a man with a funny name. One day after school, I wanted her to notice me 'out of school' and crossed the road down the Green as she was driving towards home. She noticed me, of course, and was probably annoyed with my stupidity, but didn't stop to tell me off, and didn't say anything next day, and I felt I had achieved something, though I was not sure what it was. I didn't say a word to anyone, and never noticed anyone doing the same thing, and didn't even know if Mrs Lincoln remembered.

In the big school there were two rooms. At the front end of the building was Mr Hart's classroom, with its small porch for hanging coats. You had to go through the porch to enter. Behind that porch was another, for the children of the other room. We generally ' came up' from the little school at about nine or ten years of age, so that back room had children of nine, ten, and eleven, and Mr Hart's was for the children up to fourteen, when they left. Some children were 'put up' early because of cleverness, and others could be 'kept down' for being 'slow'. In the room for the younger ones, there were two teachers, with a green curtain separating their classes. At the far end, Miss Curzon taught any children not clever enough to be with Miss Holmes. That made us think that Miss Curzon was not as clever as Miss Holmes, but she was very nice. Children who 'improved' enough might 'move up' to Miss Holmes if there was a spare seat (but by then she would be Mrs Lincoln). As in the little school, the desks were long benches with a seat attached by iron frames. There was a bar for feet, which made grit and dirt come off your soles. There could be four, five, or six children to a desk. You had to be careful not to slide sideways when a desk was empty, because if the wood was too grainy you could get a sliver in your bum.

I sometimes saw Miss Curzon when we were not at school. She was friendly with Miss Spiers who worked for Aunt Gee, serving behind the counter in her shop. Both ladies liked to be friendly and jokey with my dad, laughing, smiling through their spectacles. Perhaps Miss Spiers got to know him because the foundry workshop was next to Aunt Gee's, with just the shared yard between. He would go into the shop for tobacco.

One year, Miss Curzon knitted him a bathing costume. I didn't know why this happened, but it seemed a jokey thing to do. He was amused about it at home. It was not the usual navy blue or black but a beautiful royal blue. There was much amusement when he tried it on at Pakefield. It was knitted in the wrong kind of wool, and, when he came out of the sea it was hanging down between his legs.

I ran down the Council Road from partway up the Green near the big oak tree, dragging a light branch with many twigs and leaves. Scamp, Aunt Violet's little brown-and-white terrier, was loving it, yapping , and darting forward, in toward the scraping twigs and leaves, and out again, to have the fun of it over and over, and I ran faster to make him more excited, but it was a daft thing to do, because I did not think a car might come and kill him, but it did, and it was my fault, and nobody needed to tell me that, and I would always know it, and want to forget what I had done, and would not forget it, but would forget what happened afterwards and what Aunt Violet said or could have said to me, and what I said to anyone, except, 'I never thought' -- and knew I should have done.

When we said we were going 'down the holes', we meant we were going to a part of the Green between Rod Alley and Sunnyside. The 'holes' were large dips in the ground where clay had been dug out for centuries for cottage building. Now, the place was covered by grass and trees, so the dips and mounds made a good place to be when we didn't want to be watched.

Around some of the trees, blackberry bushes had grown. The largest had a way into its centre, the 'tunnel' as we called it, where we broke off brambles to make a passage. At the inner end of the tunnel, we cleared enough space to stand, close to the tree. This part was called 'the cave'. The cave was a place to feel safe, for planning and plotting, for just feeling good in the company of friends. When we were on our own, or perhaps with only one friend, we sometimes used the cave as a privy. We did this with easy excuses like being too far from home, but getting riled if we thought there had been a visit by someone who had no right to be in 'our' cave.

That cave ended badly. One Guy Fawkes Night, somebody set the bush alight.

Sometimes old trees around the Green had a similar ending, thrilling to watch, but with a touch of uncertainty in the pleasure. Our bush was almost gone when the flames were put out. Dad was angry at this fire being started, because the tree at the centre was too good to lose. As a young man was about to throw on a car tyre, Dad clouted him and he sidled away, muttering.

Most willow trees were tall. One day I climbed far up, and, coming down, I fell, and lay a long time, 'winded', and wondering if I would die.

Hart's way of caning was to make you hold out your hands, one after the other, and to slash them viciously, making each hand be held out again until he had finished. We called it 'getting the cosh'. After the first set of strokes it was impossible to hold out a hand again, so he ordered it to be raised, or even steadied it with his own hand. He enjoyed what he did, and enjoyed letting other teachers see him doing it. Everyone thought he was vile.

When he was not holding the cosh he was still using it, because he left it where it could be seen by everyone in his class, on the front of his desk, or on the front of a shelf in a cupboard left open. Often, he walked around the room with the cosh in his hand, taking slashes at legs that happened to stray sideways from a desk. Sometimes he asked a question and made the answer deserve punishment. Everyone knew that he enjoyed having his power over us and would not be able to go through any day without hurting someone.

There were certain boys who were coshed so often that they did not expect anything other than this. One of the most fearful things was that he often slashed the cane on the flat of a desk so it split at the end and gave greater pain. The adults in the village knew about his behaviour, but it seemed that there was nobody who dared to face him with an accusation. Some had suffered under him as children. Somebody said there was a schools inspector who protected Hart from criticism. I knew his name.

There was another person I didn't like. 'Old Nixon' with his popping-out eyes like 'glass alleys', and his antiseptic fingers pulling at my mouth, said I needed 'a filling'. He told my mother, who was in a seat just inside the door. We were in the dentist's caravan, outside Hart's school. She was as scared as I was, secretly. I was shivering. Old Nixon started up his drill, with his foot on the treadle, like someone on a one-pedal bike, or like Dad on his treadle in the workshop, working the drill for wood and metal there. As Nixon told me 'Open wide', I turned my head away in fear.

'Do that again, I'll send you in to Mr Hart,' Old Nixon said.

Mum said something. I don't know what.

He held my chin in his bony grip. His hand was stinky. His old leg pumped away. He seemed all hunched-up, on one side, balanced on one leg, his old drill whirring and grinding, 'hurting like hell', like people say. I tried to moan, but not much came. I thought of Mum, so scared. She might tell him 'Stop'. But I knew she couldn't.

'Spit that out,' he said. There was a silvery basin on the chair-arm. I wasn't silvery inside. I spat, and spat again, and dribbled noisily.

'Rinse out.' He held some coloured water in a glass.

When he had looked inside again, and turned my head about, he said, 'The next part's easy. Open wide, and wider now.'

He finished off the job, and we climbed down his steps.

'Say "Thank you, Mr Nixon", John,' Mum said. I said it. 'Thank you, Mr Nixon,' Mum said again. Someone else's mother stood there. Mum said it was dinner time, and took me home.

A short way inside the foundry yard from the door near Uncle Harry's yard, there was a wooden building called 'the office'. It was never used as an office in the time I knew it but had probably been a place where business visitors were taken, or workmen were paid wages. Now, it was grubby and untidy, its board floor never cleaned, its bench covered with small tools and scraps. Outside the door was a corrugated-iron roof, sheltering a very early Ford. I never asked about it and nobody ever said anything about its past. My mother had told me that Uncle Harry was the first man in Old Buckenham to own a car. This old Ford seemed to show that my grandfather had not been far behind his brother.

Nearby, was a Dr Harvey apple tree which seemed taller than all the trees in the orchard because it had no low branches. We either had to wait for apples to fall or to knock them down with cudgels. In their brownish roughness, they looked different from any other apples, and were my favourites.

At the side of the foundry wall, beyond the narrow path to the yard door, were two old privies, back to back, smelly and neglected. In the ground beside them was a hole covered by thick planks, where the stuff below the seats could occasionally be pushed aside to rot. Once, I was careless when needlessly crossing these, my foot parted them and went into the filth.

In the privies, the wooden seats were grey with age. The wood had never been varnished. If I sat on one, it was in the privy facing across the yard, more hidden than the other, which would be the first thing seen by anyone coming in through the gate from Uncle Harry's place. I used to think the one I used was for the men who worked for Grandad and that the other was for himself and perhaps for Dad and Uncle Leslie when they couldn't be bothered to go all the way over to their own back yards. What I supposed may not have been true, but the one I thought was for the workmen was the only privy I'd seen them go into or come from.

There was torn newspaper on the seat, to wipe your bum, or sometimes read. You could leave the door a little way open, for the light and air. There was a chronic smell or stink from down below.

'Chronic' was a word Mum used a lot. It was mostly used about things wrong with you, the ones that don't quickly go away, like coughs or aches. People often had 'chronic catarrh'. For a very long time, I didn't know what it was. I thought it was a smell.

'What do you think of this?' Grandad held up a postcard, with his finger near a name. 'Sir Malcolm Campbell: his signature.'

There was some fountain pen writing that looked like 'Malcolm', then a very big capital C and the rest inside it, just about. Grandad didn't say why he had it. I didn't ask. I used to be like that, not asking, wishing afterwards I had, but being just the same next time. I thought it would have been a gold-nib fountain pen.

I had read the story in Dad's *Daily Express*. Sir Malcolm Campbell broke the world land speed record in Bluebird, at Bonneville in Florida, at just over 301 miles per hour..

'Jibber' had sore eyes, or perhaps they weren't sore but just sore-looking. Sometimes, they were 'runny'. We liked him, but we called him 'Jibber' and nobody knew why. There were some things we said like that, but not knowing why. His name was really Geoffrey.

We noticed that the new Jubilee seat was not being used by many people. Sometimes a person waiting for a bus might sit there for a few minutes, but the buses were always on time, so there was not much need. Then, on summer evenings, and at weekends, the older lads, home from work, and wanting to be with their friends, would gather around the seat. Most were on bikes.

They mostly stayed on their bikes, one foot on a pedal, the other on the slatted Jubilee seat. They stayed for hours, some making off, others arriving. They were noisy and happy, laughing, shouting to passers-by or someone departing. None of them sat on the seat.

If you were younger, you might stand a little way off, and imagine being older. In time, you might go nearer.

By swapping something with someone, or by someone giving, I got a few old coins. One said 'George II' round the edge, and showed the king's head. I hoped to get a George I, but instead I got something better, even though it wasn't older. It was a very large, and very heavy, George III penny, with the king's head a coppery colour because it had been rubbed very smooth over the years, to stand out against the darker surround. The edges too were smooth and rounded by all the hands or other coins rubbing in pockets or purses or money-bags since eighteen-ninety-something.

The more coins you had, the more likely it was that you would notice that, whenever there was a change of king or queen, the head on the coin would be looking in a different direction. George III was looking to the right, so George II had been facing left. George IV was looking left too, and William IV looked right, before Queen Victoria looked left.

Beryl Sizeling was a girl in the big school. I did not know her well or see her much, and she died suddenly. We were all shocked and sad, and fearful, because she had caught scarlet fever, which anyone was likely to catch because 'there was a lot of it about', the grown-ups said.

Beryl lived with her aunt, Mrs Lancaster, in a little cottage next to the churchyard. It made you think that they didn't have far to take her, which was a thought that was somehow scary. All I could remember of her after a while was a very pale, sad face.

In Uncle Harry's wood, the trees were oak. I thought he must have planted them when he was young. If I had thought again, I would have known this was not true. His dad or grandad must have planted them—they'd grown too tall for Uncle Harry's time alone. They filled the far side of the Green, Mill Corner to the Banham road, hid Frost's shop and bakery, the cottages, and Hilton's farm. Oddly, they never lured us to them like the other trees, the willows 'down the holes', around the Ottermer or Rod Alley pits. We couldn't climb or swing on them, no birds built nests among their leaves. They stood, just being 'Uncle Harry's wood', the far side of Old Buckenham Green.

A lady from Scotland came to stay with us for a few days. She was a sister of Aunt Stella, Uncle Percy's wife. She believed in spirits, invisible, all around us. They were able to speak in some people's heads. They spoke in hers. To show us how this was true, she told us how a voice spoke to her in her head as she was walking alongside a road back in Scotland, and told her to cross over the road and she would

find a shilling on the ground. She crossed --
and there, at the edge of the path, she looked
down and picked up a shilling. I thought that
it must have been the voice of God. .

Alan Gedge came down the Council Road
on his bike. Near Rod Alley, perhaps he was
thinking of something that made him careless,
because he fell off, with a shout, front wheel
gone sideways, handlebars turned up. He stayed
on the road a few moments, and looked around
as he got to his feet. His bike was near enough
to kick. He kicked it, over and over, making
angry little crying noises as he kicked, until
he'd paid it out for making him fall off. Then he
looked round. He picked up the bike, straddled
the wheel he'd kicked, and straightened the
handlebar. There were a few bent spokes, I
guessed. He mounted again, swung across the
road, and pedalled away.

CHAPTER 14

'Cawston's Meetings' were where we came to be taught Bible things. We went to the meetings in the Foresters' Hall, which was a room at the side of the White Horse, because our mothers thought we should go. We learned about the Bible every day in school, often having to learn the words 'by heart'. We went to Sunday school twice every week, morning and afternoon. We went to church at eleven o'clock on Sunday, and heard the old Reverend Henry Anderson gabble his prayers and preach a sermon. But all of this was not sufficient to make sure that we were good enough in this world or likely to be chosen for the next one.

Mr Cawston and his daughter could help us to be better people by coming to their meetings to hear about God's Will and the afterlife, and of the dreadful consequences of our ignorance and evil thoughts and wrong ways. If there was any comforting thing we could discover about all that could await us in this life or the next, it was only that every one of us was likely to be 'found wanting' on the Day of Judgment. Once, Miss Cawston brought a visitor to talk to us, a man who cared for us so much that he had to beg us to bear in mind the consequences of our wrongdoing.

'If I die tonight, I know where I am going. If Miss Cawston dies tonight, she knows where she will go. But if you die tonight, do you know where you may go? Think about that.'

Sometimes we were given booklets to take home, to scare us between meetings. They told of such things as people like someone called Voltaire being, on his deathbed, finally sorry for all his sins and asking God's forgiveness.

The chances of being one of the Chosen were so small that there was no help to be found in the company of our friends. We did not even think of them in the face of what we would have to suffer. We discovered one way of making a small break in the awful seriousness. Early in meetings, when we had to answer to our names being called for the register, we had to say 'present', and Miss Cawston would give us a mark in the book. A best moment was when John Bray dared to say 'pheasant' instead, and Miss Cawston did not notice. Another was when my grandfather told me that Mr Cawston owed him seventy pounds on his threshing bill, and had owed it for a long time.

We often called John Bray 'Hinney' Bray. I don't know why and I don't think any of us did. One day I heard him say a word differently from all the rest of us. We all knew it should be 'shed', but Hinney said, 'I go in my father's "shud". Nobody asked him why he said it like that. He would have said, 'Because tha's the way it should be!' I thought it must be the way his dad said it. I wondered if it was an old Norfolk way.

'Wiggy' Westfield was a name we liked to say. Nobody would have thought of saying 'Mister' Westfield, except to his face or to Mrs Westfield or their daughter, Marjorie We didn't know much about Wiggy, because he was always at work, hidden in his garage, only coming out at the occasional pulling up of a car beside his petrol pump. We mainly used the little shop, where his wife or daughter served, for buying sweets or batteries, or cigarettes and tobacco for parents. Wiggy Westfield's corner was the place to cross the road, opposite to Bye's general shop, much larger than Westfield's.

Bye's shop, with Mrs Bye, a thin lady in thick spectacles, who had to cross the floor between her two counters, always seemed to be waiting for customers who didn't come. When she got them, she might need to serve from both counters. Arthur Bye seemed to have time to spare. I never knew what work he did, and didn't ask anyone. Perha[s he found jobs that needed doing in the back of the shop, like unpackung the goods, and ordering more. Sometimes he went to Aunt Violet's tennis court at Sunnyside, and mowed the grass, then rolled the court with the biggest roller in the village, made from the barrel of an old steam engine. It had a heavy handle, which would have been too heavy to lift if it had not been balanced by a great weight of iron fixed to its ends inside the roller. It was good fun, when nobody was looking, to pull the handle down, leave go, and see it fly up.

One day when Alfred Etteridge and I bowled hoops, we crossed from Wiggy's side to Bye's just as a car came from the Attleborough direction. I felt the mudguard touch my trousers, but Alfred tried to stop, fell backwards, and a wheel went over one of his legs, but without breaking it. One thing I thought about Alfred was how good it was for him to have an older brother, Dougie, who could do things for him he couldn't quite manage for himself.

Just past Wiggy Westfield's corner, on the first field of the farm on the left side of the Attleborough Road, there was a crop of peas. It was a good surprise to find them, watching out in case someone should come and spoil the treat of opening shells, and seeing them, green and fat, and ready for our fingers, our mouths, and our bellies, tasting better than all the peas we'd ever had before. And there was the thrill of trespassing, to make it better still

In school, Mrs Hart told us about a man called 'Turnip' Townshend who lived in the reign of King George the First. After many years in important jobs in the Government, he returned to live on his estate in Norfolk and tried to improve ways of farming. He thought of the idea of growing different crops in his fields each year, over four years, because the changes would be good for the soil, and the crops would be better. The order would be wheat, clover, barley, turnips. In the clover year, the grazing animals would be able to be in that field. Instead of turnips, any other root crops would do, but Lord Townshend used turnips, and so he got his famous nickname, and it was because of that we remember him so easily. The most usual root crop nowadays was sugar-beet, and that made some people annoyed because they were piled-up at the side of all roads, for collection by lorries, and mud was spread all over the roads for many yards.

I think the peas were only in the Stevensons' field that one year we 'pinched' them.

Peter Kemp walked by the hedge between the schools. Suddenly he fell over, collapsed into a sort of folded up boy, in need of help to be upright again, and moveable. He had something wrong with his limbs. They didn't work together and keep him balanced for walking, or even standing. He was thin. Pink knees were very noticeable between trousers and socks. We looked there, because that was where he bent. We helped him up, and he was all right, as if nothing special had happened.

He was very intelligent even though his speech was slurred. One day, when a small group was talking in the 'big' school playground, which was the part of the Green in front of the school, I said something stupid, a kind of showing-off, not intended, just happening. I said my family came from the West Indies. Nobody else commented on that, but Peter said it was not true. I said it was. He said, more strongly, that it was just not true. He could have said, 'You are lying', but he didn't, because there was no need. Everyone already believed him, and I was left feeling stupid, even though I said again that I was telling the truth. I had told what Mrs Hart called 'an untruth', and everyone knew it because of Peter being determined that things said should be true.

I went to Aunt Decima's house to read Uncle Stephen's *David Copperfield*. It was from a row of books by Dickens, all bound in brown leather. I was not allowed to take it home, but came, day after day, to their smart new house, the further side of Uncle Harry's old one, and next to Elvin's yard. The house was shining. It seemed unused. They worked with Uncle Harry, Stephen in the bakery, Aunt Decima in the shop. They were out of their house almost every day, including Sunday. They went to morning service and to evensong. There was no time to drop a crumb. They often had their meals with Aunt Gee and Uncle Harry anyway. The books were like the house, they looked unused. I had to open *David* Copperfield flat on the shining table, with clean hands.

I liked the Peggotty boat on Yarmouth Sands. It felt so close to home.

Later I had my own book, an easy-to-read one, from the film, a page of print, a picture, all the way through. The pictures told the story better than those words, and brought back the words by Dickens that had already put their pictures in my head.

Around that time, I read *Oliver Twist,* but in a book my grandmother handed-on to me. I was Oliver when he slept beneath the bench, with coffins close, and I was there with Oliver among the boys, watched Fagin's face with them, knew Nancy could be kind, was scared by Sykes, and, when the time came, sat with Fagin in his cell.

Aunt Decima's mother was Mrs Nobbs. She was a serious lady who liked to give opinions. Mum listened to her too much, Dad said. If Mum had some idea he didn't like, he sometimes said, 'That's bloody old Mrs Nobbs.' It sometimes was.

Sid Nobbs was not serious. He was an odd man, and enjoyed saying things people thought to be funny. Dad told me that when I was very small Mr Nobbs asked me, 'Does your father kiss your mother?' and I said, 'Not now, but he use-er to.' Dad liked telling that story. It made people laugh.

A British Legion fete was at Old Buckenham Hall. People came from miles around. There were sports and sideshows. The races weren't for just anyone. Athletes were real ones, runners, jumpers, cyclists. Some were good to watch awhile, but there was too much. You needed to know 'who's who', to want someone special to you to win, to cheer that someone on. But you had to know about them, more than we could know. We really didn't care much who won. But it all looked expert and we were proud it was happening where we lived. Sometimes there was someone who looked different, who looked like someone to be liked and cheered, someone who smiled at you. Sideshows were better, if you had the money for a go. I never seemed to win. Once there was a fancy dress parade. I went in with a cowboy suit, a bought one, not so good as my Indian clothes Aunt Ethel made. There is a photograph. I'm nine, look daft a bit. Someone must have told me 'Point your gun', so I stand there pointing it, head on one side as if to ask them, 'Is this right?' In the background, there are Podger Fisk and Alma Beales. Alma is supposed to be Chinese. And she looks good.

A biplane came down on a field, beyond a line of pine trees. People went through there for rides. One old lady went. She was over eighty. Some people said, 'She's a brave old girl.' Some said 'Daft.'

Whenever there were events at Oldd Buckenham Hall, someone was likely to remember that, in the days when the millionaire Lionel Robinson owned the Hall, the Australian Test Match cricket team had come here to play a match against a local team organised by Mr Robinson.

'You ought to show that to Mr Hart,' my mother said. So I showed my poem. It was not a good idea. He read, said nothing, handed it back. It was just after school. Mrs Lincoln and Miss Curzon were with him near the fireguard.

'Do you have broccoli?' he said.

'Yes, sir.' I thought he'd said, 'Do you have a rockery?'

He sensed a lie, but was not sure

'All right. Off you go.'

What he had really said was quickly clear, but it didn't explain what broccoli was. I found out later. He was offering what might go to waste from the small school garden plot a few yards down Church Lane. The boy was stupid or had lied. He made a comment as I went.

'He's a mother's boy.'

They hadn't read the poem anyway.

There was a short while when I was not so much Red Indian or a 'Westerner'. For a few weeks, or it could have been a few days spread over weeks, I became a detective. The change was caused by an advertisement somewhere, probably on a cornflake packet, for a set of detective equipment you could get by sending for it and paying for the postage. So I had a tiny magnifying-glass, for examining finger-prints and other clues, and a booklet about detective work. The best thing was a little black 'seebacroscope', made of Bakelite, with a hole at the back to put your eye against, and see, inside, a tiny mirror, slightly at angle, so it showed, through another hole, an image of the person following you, who was likely to be the 'crook', that you would be following later, which seemed more likely when we thought a bit. It would be more exciting if you said 'trailing' instead of 'following', which was more like a detective talking. Whether detectives from 'The Yard' used a seebacroscope, we didn't know, and the booklet didn't say, but we could assume they did, and so we dreamed a while of being from New Scotland Yard, and read of how to 'investigate', and walk past Edgar Sparrow's blacksmith's place with your eye on the mirror, ready for someone to come in view, though nobody did, and after you had read the booklet several times, and knew enough about 'sleuthing', you galloped away into some prairie distance once again, or sometimes changed you mind, because there was a penny in your pocket.

'Golden Charm?' asked Mrs Moore. The chocolate-toffee jar already had the lid off as you came in.

Mr George Kettle came back from the Great War with a wooden leg. He went stomp, stomp to work from Mrs Beales' house behind Hart's school. His work was cobbling, which was mending boots and shoes. He had a little wooden hut, near Bloom's, the grocery shop, and Uncle Dick's, butcher's. He perched upon a wooden stool to do it all, the cutting leather, sewing it, hammering the nails in soles. Anyone could see him there. He always smiled when you came near. The door was mostly open wide, so he could see the people come and go. Some liked to stay a while to talk. George liked to talk, but what he liked especially, was listening. His visitors would stand there ages, telling what they had to tell. I never knew him not to smile when I came with my shoes, or came to get them back when they were done. George shut his door at evening, went stomping to his lodgings, home.

Mr Murdstone used a cane on David Copperfield. He was a man like Hart. I hated him, was happy when he rode his donkey on Miss Betsy Trotwood's lawn, and she laid into him with a stick. 'It served him right,' was what we said when someone got what they deserved.

We liked people getting what they deserved, if it wasn't us.

'Who done that?' someone asked.

Reggie said, 'Old Prick' It was something he said when there was really no answer. It didn't seem someone real, just a name to say for a joke. Old Prick could be blamed for anything. You soon began to understand it was a bit rude, and tried saying it yourself.

Grandad held out a book for me to look at. It was new, with a creamy-white cover, with a drawing of a bunch of cherries and a title, *Buy Your Own Cherries*. When I opened it, I thought it didn't seem a very interesting story, because no words jumped up to your eyes, as they do in good stories. They all stayed there in their places, ready for reading, and I knew I didn't want to read them. Grandad noticed. He started to tell me how he had bought the book from a lady who came to the back door. She was selling it because it was a book of good advice about how people should live their lives. After he said that, his hand was out to take it, and I handed it back without knowing what to say.

'... about being sensible and honest, and all that sort of thing,' he was saying.

I said yes. I thought Grandad didn't need a book to tell him about honesty. He was as honest as anyone could be. Mum often said old sayings: 'as honest as they come', 'as honest as the day is long'.

So I never read *Buy Your Own Cherries,* and I didn't know whether he read it all the way through. He would have bought his own cherries anyway.

In twos and threes, late afternoon, men bike past Rod Alley pit. Some turn down Abbey Road, some go right, and past the threshing things, some go on up the Council Road to Banham or New Buckenham. They come from Gaymer's cider works, crank home, bent over handlebars, against the wind or weariness. Some are on their Great War bikes, some in khaki greatcoats, still not worn out, and even if they are, still good against the cold. Eighteen years have gone now since the war. The names of those who were killed are on the Memorial opposite the 'little school'. In spring the daffodils are thick around. The men on bikes are the lucky ones. You can't believe how many names are there. One says 'Charles Loveday, 2nd Lieutenant, Machine Gun Corps'. My middle name was Charles because Dad wanted me to have his oldest brother's name.

One Sunday, I was standing near Grandad's chair as he sat at his desk. He was looking out, up the left-hand edge of the Green. The church bells were ringing people to the evening service.

'I hate them bells,' he said.

CHAPTER 15

Dad threshing: you could hear the chuffing sound of the engine and the grumble of the drum from a good way off, and see the smoke puff up. The drum and straw pitcher were brightly coloured, yellow mostly, with parts red or green. Seeing them in a field was always exciting, set away in a corner, white smoke against trees, spreading against the sky. Nearer, you could see the men on the stacks, pitchforks moving in rhythm, sheaves pitched to the man on the drum, the busiest man of all, only his head and shoulders seen as he stood in his low place, feeding sheaves to the drum. As one stack was losing its sheaves, the other, at the far end of the straw pitcher, was rising, straw dropping to more men with pitchforks. On the engine, or never far away, you would see Dad. His other place might be a corner of the drum where grain poured to a sack on hooks. He could carry a full one on his back, men said.

Corn field, the sun well down, the brown-armed men, the binder homing in, the cudgel in my hand, the moment when, blindly, the rabbits run: gladly, I never caught one, would have panicked at the poor maimed struggler, not held it right, bungled the blow to kill.

'Harvest holidays' was what we called the school summer holiday. It was a good time to watch the threshing. Often there was no corn stack. The sheaves were pitched to the drum from a wagon, while horses waited, swishing tails, shaking heads and harness, impatient to be off with an empty wagon, making way for a wagon with a load that looked too high for safety.

An old army bike leans into a bush, and into the shadows it makes by being there. Birds chirp. There is a bag made of sacking, slung from the side-turned handlebar, bulging with a two-pint cider-bottle of cold tea and the shape of a tin box of sandwiches for 'elevenses' and 'dinner-time'. It hangs down to touch the top of the front wheel, just into the sunlight there. Now, the engine's chuffing has stopped, the drum's sounds too. A man with rolled-up sleeves, and 'binder-twine' tied round the bottom of his trouser-legs, goes behind the bush to pee. The string is round his trousers so rats from the stack can't run up inside.

Harvest holidays, and no more Hart, no more 'wrong' sums, or making table mats with raffia every afternoon, no more blots on pages, no more rulers, no more cosh, no more 'Our Father chart in Heavun', no more 'going round the back', no more worrying about next day, no more, no more anything like that. Five lovely, long weeks, and the day in September was a long, long time away, away, not quite forever but near enough. On the coal box lid behind the bungalow at Pakefield, the dustbin lid beside it, hot in the daylong sun, the 'sixteen acre' bushes, good for play, like 'the holes' at home, and Russell's friends, George and Ronnie, and Jeffery (who warned I shouldn't wear my new blue shirt, it should have been washed first, his mother said), and Uncle George's corrugated iron garage, where he kept his bicycle and did his carpentry and came in from at dinner time and sometimes said a little sharply 'Shut that duzzy door' (the one into the hallway) and we did.

'Don't be nesh,' Aunt Mabel said. She was telling Russell and me that we shouldn't be afraid of doing things that should be done. I hadn't heard anyone use that word before, but could guess what it meant. I thought it was an old one she had 'picked up'.

I had a second-hand bike when I was eight. Dad painted it green, and straight away it seemed mine, as if it had never been anyone else's. Soon, it seemed we had been together for ages. Sometimes, at the end of the day, I'd lie in bed and think what the bike and I had been through together. I even talked to it in imagination, saying what we had done. 'The trouble was', as you often heard people say, that I was getting bigger and the bike stayed as it was. But it always liked what I said.

Cookie, who worked around the threshing machines, could ride his bike faster than I could ride mine. We didn't race, but I just knew from when we rode together and keeping up was hard but never to be mentioned. He had one good leg. The other was there, but always bent. Being expert on a bike was Cookie's way of showing that the crookedness was of no great bother. When I was ten, he was about thirty. I lived in an ordinary sort of house. He lived in a corrugated iron hut on iron wheels.

Everybody thought Cookie was odd and a bit rough (very rough, to tell it truly) but everybody liked him. He was always grinning, his face weather-beaten, his hair an uncombed, unwashed yellow. His showing-off was mostly of things we wondered at but never wanted to do. His leg was able to take his firewood snapped across it. His teeth could have a three inch nail bent to a curve. His special trick was suddenly to stand up tall on one good leg, the other dangling, to show, if just for laughs, what might have been.

Cookie's name was Sidney: Sidney Cook. But nobody called him that, unless my mother did, once or twice. I think it on her voice: 'Hello, Sidney'. Yes, that's true. How strange to be just 'Cookie', and good too. We just said 'Cookie'. He liked that. He grinned, liked us to like him. It was in the way we said it. There were Sidneys everywhere.

I never knew why Cookie had his bad leg. He didn't talk about it, and we didn't ask him. There were several men, like George Kettle, who got wounded in the Great War, but Cookie was not one of them. Billy Goodrum, who worked the mill, lost his right arm in the machinery there. We thought of him as 'Billy with one arm'. He still managed his mill somehow, but nowadays it was driven by an engine, not the sails, which were old and damaged, looking forlorn.

My dad's injuries from work were small, but they came back over and over, red, bare knuckles, usually from knocks by a hammer or some other tool. He thought of them as something to be expected in his job. The dirt getting on them from engine coal and oil made them worse, but there was no way round the problem.

A different kind of wound, from the Great War, was not seen as often as people said it had been in the first few years after the war. Some men had been 'shell-shocked' by the explosions around the trenches in France. They couldn't stop having shivering fits, or shouting out oddly, or bursting into tears. Others, or sometimes the same men, had been overcome by poison gas, and still could not breathe properly. We did not see any of the worst of these wounds, because men had slowly got a bit better. But some had died, sometimes after several years.

In Attleborough, there was a man they called 'Umbrella Joe'. He spent his time walking the streets, endlessly retracing his footsteps, always with his umbrella used as a walking stick, talking to people, talking to himself, saying the same words over and over, looking odd, so that people who didn't know him might laugh. People who knew him might also be amused when they talked of seeing him.

People talked about soldiers who had been in India, even long ago, and had come home with the 'Dulali-tap' It was being 'not right in the head' because of a kind of fever from the heat that left them changed. Dulali was the name of just one of the places in which it happened.

There is a wound on my hand that will always be there, a white scar on my left thumb, halfway down. I was in the pantry, which was behind the door in the right-hand corner, matching the door on the other side of the fireplace, into the scullery. At the inner end of the pantry, near a small window over the back garden, there was a wooden cupboard with a panel of zinc in its door, so food inside could have fresh air, with flies kept out. This was where our meat was kept. Rats also liked meat, so the cupboard was high, about the height of my shoulders when I was six or seven. You would not think a rat could get in there, but one rat did, by scraping, gnawing up inside the house wall from the Sturmans' garden side. A hole came in a corner of the cupboard. Dad set a trap. I didn't know. I opened the door, but have no idea why I put my hand inside. The trap snapped shut. I have this scar.

My cousin Olive looked like the most famous girl in the world. Olive's face was pretty, but it was the ringlets in her hair made people look at her. Aunt Mabel worked at them, tying them tight at bedtime so that in the morning they would stay in place, a mass of ringlets round her head, the Shirley Temple look. Over the world, people went to the 'picture house' to see it. Shirley Temple could act well too, and that made all the difference, but people who want to imitate don't think of that. The fact that, then, I couldn't even ride a horse would never keep me from a picture house where Hopalong Cassidy was on.

So Olive went on looking splendid, but, on holiday in Rod Alley Row, she asked my mum to cut her ringlets off. She had grown tired of them. She wanted pretty ringlets round her head no more. Mum wasn't sure what she should do, but took her scissors out in sympathy. Olive was pleased to see the ringlets gathered neatly in a golden pile. She still looked quite as good as Shirley did, and as she wished. But what Aunt Mabel thought when she went home is not part of the story. I didn't hear it said.

'He's pissed hisself,' loud Doreen said.

A small group stood on the Green. I looked down at the tiny point of darkness.

'He has not.' Olive said it as if she said 'Shut up.' I treasured her, as always.

We talked of something I don't remember. This was at the time when I was thinking I was too old for dressing up. Boys of ten should look like boys of ten, not Red Indians. The clothes were splitting. Mum sewed up seams, then gave the needle and thread to me. I left them off, the Indian clothes, their make-believe.

Grey Owl wrote stories of animals in the forests of America. I longed to read his books, but had to 'make do' with what the newspapers told. My books had mostly come as gifts, not often new, and none was by Grey Owl. In much the same way, I wanted a book by Lawrence of Arabia, or one about him, but had to want.

Grey Owl went talking round the country, and was talked about, with pictures in the papers, loved by people who loved Red Indian lore. Newspapers said that he was not Indian, but Archibald Belany, Englishman. He was still Grey Owl, anyway.

Cheyenne, Navajo, Arapaho, Sioux ... I knew some Indian tribes. Blackfoot, Cherokee, Apache, Crow ... But there were many, many more I didn't know.

In an 'annual', a story slipped out of my mind quite soon, but the picture for it stayed, in colour and bright light. An Indian holding a bow, at the top of a deep ravine, looked down upon a traveller who did not know that he was watched by someone with the power to kill. The book always opened at that page.

''Faint heart never won fair lady,' Mum said. It was nothing to do with a fair lady, but just a way of encouraging me not to be nervous about something I should do. It was the same as Aunt Mabel saying 'Don't be nesh', or Uncle Dick saying 'Don't let your mother think she had a jibber'. It was all meant to be helpful advice. But to think of a fair lady seemed about something a long way off, so far ahead that it was not real. It was like something in a story book. So the way Maid Marian seemed to Robin Hood was good to think about, but it was only a quickly-passing sort of thought.

Another night of wind, this wind. A willow is down in the pit. We rush to it with ,'You be careful, be careful, do you hear?' behind. We are all over it, the first-time-ever excitement making us move across and back and across again, out on branches, in each other's way, until we're tired, and stilled a bit, and happy a bit, and even sorry for the tree a bit. And next day it will be a good thing still, but in a different way.

The willow is left because it is a busy time for engines in the fields. Then a day comes for dragging it away for the sawbench, and the long white planks under corrugated iron, and new sawdust on the heap in a corner of the orchard. A long wire rope winds out from the back of the engine. Dad and Uncle Leslie fix it around the tree. Dad goes back to the engine. The engine puffs and chuffs, and smoke makes quick, black clouds, the wire rope tightens and winds in, with branches dragging, slashing and splashing as the trunk is taken, bottom-first, through the pit, and out at the Green end, up the slope where the cows come down, across the road and on to the grass, a few people looking on admiring, pleased, and sad because the something different is over.

The fallen tree has gone. The pit is just a pit again. We stand around, looking at the dangerous depths, missing the thrill of moving across the bridge it had become. Walking the trunk was a challenge for balancing, and nobody fell in. The branches gave a tangle of new places to discover in safety, footholds and handholds together, testing of springiness, trying out of ways around, of reliability, unreliability, and your own judgement of both, and of your own courage or fear, of imagining, imagining – and never without the background of the water that goes down, down, down, as the old stories say.

CHAPTER 16

'Which side would you have been on in the English Civil War?' Uncle Oliver asked. He was back at Sunnyside for a few days. I said the Cavaliers'. He smiled, but said I would have been wrong. He explained how Cromwell and the Roundheads had the better ideas for good government, and that the beginnings of change would never have come from the Royalist side. I liked his way of facing me with serious questions and assuming I would understand his more difficult words, which I did, mainly. But, at the same time, I felt regret at the loss of a romantic king and his soldiers. This was my first experience of being asked to consider an adult kind of question.

'Mind you don't strain y' fartin' clappers,' Reggie said.

Whatever we were trying to do, we would be likely to stop, and laugh instead. Reggie liked to be with boys younger than he was. He could show us how much he knew.. He could tell us things we didn't know. And, most of all, he could make us laugh.

We didn't know where he learned the things he said. The word 'clappers' seemed the wrong word, because it made you imagine the wrong sound. But it was also funny, so we liked saying it over.

Our little dog called Brownie was buried under the largest apple tree, at the back of the orchard. Dad put a block of wood against the fence, with his name. He was killed on the road on a day I was not at home, and Dad had done all the caring for him by the evening.

There are lost things we don't forget. There was a model boat, brown, with sails and rigging. I launched it on to the Rod Alley pit and watched it move away. But it became becalmed, out of reach from anywhere around. After a while, it seemed a disappointing plaything, unmoving for some reason I could not make out. I went indoors at evening, only partly caring if I never saw it again, and I never did.

Once, near a blackberry bush, I found a boy who was pushing hispenknife, down the throat of a baby bird he had taken from its nest. His best friend was with him. The little bird's mouth was wide open, as if it was ready to be fed, with its bright yellow edging of beak. I couldn't look any more. I shall not tell their names because what they were enjoying was terrible. They knew that and would never do it again.

In the excitement of our play, sometimes, we imitated what we had seen in the 'picture house'. A boy was running, I was chasing him, holding my air gun by its barrel, swinging it as I got close. It hit him on the side of his head, not solidly, but I was scared, at the thought of the damage nearly caused.

'Take a robin's egg: you'll get a broken leg.' We really believed in that. One year, a little way down Abbey Road, there was a mossy nest high in the hedge on the left-hand side. How we found it, I don't know. It was above our heads. We had to reach and hold on, so we could just look into it to see five tiny eggs, faint bluey-grey, with mottled brown. We always said the words and knew we'd leave them. Even touching wasn't allowed. They might be broken, which would count as taking or even worse. We just 'let them be'. The robins would know they'd been touched anyway, might leave the nest, and the little things inside the shells would die. We played a bit, down in the ditch, the other side of the narrow road. Primroses grew there on the banks, low down. None of us ever had a broken leg.

You could make a collection of other bird's eggs, and keep them in a flat box, in little nests of cotton-wool your mother would give you, or a piece of folded cloth. But, first, you would have to 'blow' them. This was to get the inside stuff out, so your egg collection didn't go rotten. An older boy would show you how. Reggie showed me. You took a straight pin and pushed it through the shell, top and bottom, very, very carefully, so as to make the holes without cracking it. When that was done, all the yolk and the runny stuff around it was ready to come out. But to get it out you have to blow gently into the top hole. It usually took several tries, which meant several broken eggs, before you were expert. Not many boys built up big collections, but you always thought you would, at the start. Most of us didn't get further than the common ones, blackbirds, pigeons, sparrows, thrushes.

'Red hat and no drawers,' people said about some lady, and it seemed lovely-and-rude, and something we could show we were amused about.

'He can't tell his arse from his elbow.'

It was said when someone seemed stupid. We loved to hear grown-ups say rude things too, so they seemed like us. But there were some who never did it. Mum said they were 'strait-laced' or 'stuck-up'. She didn't like them. She thought the aunts from Sunnyside were like that, except Aunt Violet. Aunt Ethel thought so too.

An old Fiat stood in a space cleared for it at the inner end of the woodshed. It was Uncle Leslie's car, and he was proud of it. It was dullish red, and had a canvas hood that folded back. It was the only Fiat I knew, and seemed something to be proud of, because of being unusual. I didn't know how Uncle Leslie got his Fiat, and didn't ask him. I wish I had, because he would have been proud to talk about it. I was a bit careful never to do anything to annoy Uncle Leslie because he didn't smile much. I thought he looked as if he was annoyed already, so I mustn't make it worse. I remembered saying, 'That's Uncle Leslie!' to Aunt Violet, about Giant Decay in the board game, and how annoyed she was. But I was pleased that there seemed something special about a Fiat, and glad that my Uncle Leslie had one.

When Dad was a young man, still living at Sunnyside, he had a little Morgan car. It was a three-wheeler, dark red, with a canvas hood that folded back for good weather. There was a photograph of Dad sitting in it, smiling and proud, near the iron railings of the orchard. It was a two-seater, with a space at the back for luggage or a small person. In the photograph, the seat beside Dad was empty, and whenever it was shown someone was sure to tell the story of how Aunt Violet had fallen out as Dad sped round a corner. Whether the door had opened, or she had gone over the top of it, was not clear, but she was uninjured.

‑‑‑‑❦‑‑‑‑

'I know what you're doing.' It was a girl's voice.

Some of the boys in the small circle might not have recognized it, but I knew instantly it was my cousin Beryl, and reached up slightly from the tall grasses near the orchard. She stood some way off. I knew she couldn't see much from there, but was alarmed that her guess was right.

'We aren't doing anything,' I said.

The little pink cocks, all timid and ready to be hidden, had already gone, in a scramble of putting away and buttoning, and the pretence of innocence.

'We wasn't doin' nothin', a couple of voices said.

'I know what you're doing,' she said again. Her voice was unexcited. It was not going to tell anyone. She was just pleased to keep the secret. But she liked the advantage it gave her over us. She would not come nearer. She could only go away. She had not actually seen anything. It was possible she saw in secret from a different angle, just as we started. Reggie's was out first. Perhaps she saw it, a bit ruder, a bit more used to being looked at, but nothing she would tell of.

When she went, we no longer had the excitement of showing, and perhaps we were glad. But something had happened that was more than had happened before. It was a day of no great difference from any other, but we would remember it.

CHAPTER 17

A little rising road turns left before the Stacksford corner where Hart lives. A patch of grass makes the turning point. A walnut tree, only a few years old, grows at the centre of the triangle. With Chum, there is a while for us to carve initials in smooth bark, CL, JL. He likes us doing that. There can't be much chance of carving initials where he comes from. We think our marks will be there for as long as this tree grows, for all our lives and more. Then we go on again, but not the Stacksford way. The road goes over the stream that comes down from the Hall. It's shallow, clean, quite fast, not really fast, but fast enough. We drop a leaf or two from one side of the bridge the road goes over, and watch them come out the other side.

I've waded here. We call the stream the Stax, because that would be the reason for the name

Stacksford, where, in olden days, people forded. That way of spelling the name was shown on Hart's house. Nobody seemed to know when the change happened, nor exactly where people forded.

Now we go on to the warren, where the road is flat between two sides of bracken, gorse, and purple heather. There's a row of beeches, then more warren, but now only on one side, right hand, the Stacksford side. Beyond an uncertain point, the name is changed. It's Wilby Warren there, because, long ago, there was a body found, and Old Buckenham church people would not have it buried in their ground, but Wilby took it and, ever afterwards, claimed that part of the warren as their land. Old Buckenham people do not seem to care. Nobody comes here much. It's good to be here, crawl through bracken, hide, lie among the heather and the spongy grass, and watch the sky. When it's time to go, we know because we're getting hungry. Chum mustn't be late because he's staying with Grandma. His mother told him that, I know. The Green seems far away. We go, trudge, trudge. After the walnut tree, the slope is up. We look at our initials on the way.

A huge heap of sawdust in the far right hand corner beyond the orchard behind the foundry, looking from our back gate, was where the waste of many years of work with the two sawbenches was dumped It was a good place to be, especially at the end of a sawing day, when the scent of wood was everywhere, and we could burrow holes to lie in. Sometimes we played there, or just lay there for hours. A few yards from the sawdust heap was an old tree on which ivy had grown so thick that we simply called it the ivy tree. At the top of the trunk you could lie for the pleasure of just being there, where nobody would ever say you should not be, because it was a place nobody ever claimed or needed. What kind of tree grew beneath the ivy was never thought about. It must have been a plum tree, but no plums ever appeared.

On the far side of the sawdust heap, there was a very different plum tree, at the corner, tall and leafy, heavy with Victoria plums, on Uncle Harry's side of the corrugated fence, but close. I climbed quite high, and ate a plum, heard Uncle Harry's voice.

'Come down from there.'

Surprised and scared, I didn't, move.

'Come down from there.'

I sat and waited. He waited too. At last he said something to himself, and went. I waited a good while longer, to be sure he must have gone, and wasn't waiting further off. I didn't want another plum.

The tree could stay unclimbed. I don't know why he left, and wonder if he thought I'd gone, or hadn't been there. He could have been a bit amused. He never mentioned it, and nor did I.

There was an old army bike from the Great War. It stood in various places in the foundry yard, but nobody seemed to ride it. It was dully-painted in a light khaki colour.

I started to try it out. Even with the big leather seat right down to the cross-bar, it was still too tall for me to ride comfortably, but I was able to go from side to side, standing on the pedals, because the bike ran so smoothly that, much of the time, I hardly needed to pedal at all. If you got up speed, it would free-wheel for a very long way, much further than any bike I'd ever seen. The reason was, obviously, it was so very well made. It was good to think of so very many bikes being made so well.

There were still quite a lot of army bikes being ridden by men who had been soldiers. I guessed that they had been able to buy them cheaply when they came home from the war. There were many who wore their army great-coats too.

I also learned to do tricks on the bike. One was, to get up speed, then to get my feet up to the seat, letting one leg go out to the side to balance, with one arm raised too. It would not have been possible on any other kind of bike. You could imagine people admiring, when there wasn't anyone to notice at all.

The Ottermer pit was on the side of the Green near Hart's school. It was at the bottom of surrounding slopes, and had no steep sides. It was not very deep, even at the centre. It was a good pit for skating, even when the ice had thawed enough to bend as you skated over it. We liked all the skating, but this was the part that tested us out for courage and scaring ourselves for the thrill it gave, and the pleasure of hearing the surprise when we managed not to dare 'just once too often'. Of all the scary things we tried in any games, there was nothing to compare with feeling the ice dip as you glided over it, and seeing the bending and movement of a surface that might break and make you look foolish to the jeering onlookers who, a moment earlier, would have been envious of your skill.

I had some skates that Grandma saved for many years, from when her sons had used them. Dad brought them home. There were two pairs with steel blades set in wood. A screw at the back had to be turned into a leather boot heel, and the front strapped tightly to the boot. They were of different sizes. I liked the look of them, but they were not as good as the two other pairs. These were all-steel, the blades turned up at the front, almost in three quarters of a circle. I liked them very much. They let me glide without a fear of falling, turned without a scrape or scratch. They made you taller, looked like a man's skate, anyway. These were for the older boys. Now I was using skates Uncles Charles and Oliver had used when they were boys before the Great War. They clipped to the boot, and tightened on.

One of my early memories was of being on the Rod Alley ice with Dad when I was six. I wore the smallest of the skates, with blades in wood. My memory was of standing, holding Dad's hand. It must have been a year when ice was thick and very safe. There were other people there, skating, sliding.

Hart made me and someone else stand at the end of a long desk to wait while he decided, stick in hand, what to do with us. We were only about a yard from the door. The big latch clicked and the door opened. Reggie Elvin stood there, late for school and taken by surprise to find Hart facing him, when he had hoped to slip in without much fuss from Mrs Lincoln about his lateness. He obviously had a good excuse. His face was swollen on one side, and he looked tired and unwell.

'Late,' said Hart.

'Bin awake all night,' said Reggie. 'I got the toothache.' Then he added something stupid to say, 'You can't hit me today.'

'Can't I?' shouted Hart. He swung his arm. The flat of his hand struck Reggie full on his swollen cheek. Reggie bawled with pain.

I didn't know if Hart looked pleased with himself, because we often turned our eyes away from him. I was standing nearer to Reggie than anyone else. What Hart did was a disgrace, but not one of us would dare to tell anyone how bad it was.

We stood in a group, just talking. There was a new girl, Iris Stebbing, who looked at my sore hands and said something wise and kind. I don't remember the words, but I felt, for the first time, and coming from a girl, a special gift of tenderness that took me by surprise.

Arthur Kett was called only Kett by everyone. It was easily possible to think that it was his only name. Hart seemed to dislike him more than any other boy in the school. It might not be true to say that he caned him every day. Think of that as a slight exaggeration, because it was how it seemed. Kett seemed to have no family. He lived at the beginning of Fen Street, with a family who cared for him. But nobody did anything to protect him from Hart, and it seemed that nothing could be done. If somebody had gone to old Henry Anderson, the vicar, he might have been ashamed enough to tell Hart to stop. But nobody did. And so the story has never been told.

The only other Kett I knew of was the Norfolk man who rebelled against the king in olden days. Some of us knew the old oak tree on the Norwich road beyond Attleborough. It was called Kett's Oak. People said that was where he was hanged, but they were wrong. Kett's Oak was where his followers first gathered for rebellion. He was hanged on Norwich Castle wall, so very many more people would be scared, and be obedient. I sometimes wondered if Hart was hard on Kett at school because of his name. I always felt proud to know about the Kett in history, because he was a Norfolk man.

Once, Donnie Wilde made a swap with me. I can't remember what I gave, but he gave me a 'crystal set', which was the very first kind of 'wireless' made. There was a tiny crystal mounted on a stand, a handle with a short wire at the end, and earphones that the sound should come through when you touched the crystal with the wire. But no sound came. I tried occasionally for a while, but knew that Donnie had swapped it as a useless thing, just as some grown-up must have given it to him.

One evening I was allowed to be with Donny while his parents went out, and just before they arrived home, his sister Pauline jumped on the bedroom floor, and her foot came through the ceiling. The cottages in Churh Lane were very old

When Mum was sure that someone would have to 'change his mind' because he was being too sure about something, or boasting about what he was going to do, she would say, 'He's got another think coming'. She could have said 'another thought coming', but 'think' is better. I have 'thinks'. They come at anytime and anywhere. But in bed is one of the best places, just before going to sleep, or soon after waking up. Sometimes they start in a dream and wake you up. Sometimes you go where a think will come. In the old 'ivy tree', sitting in the hollow place at the top of the trunk, between the places where the branches used to start from, I can find any thinks I like to have. You could say 'thoughts', but that sounds not so real. Thinks are very real, even when I am imagining, like how good I could be as a boxer one day. They are so real you can punch them. You can love them, hate them, laugh at them, listen to them, chuck them about. They just keep coming. When I am reading, it is just the author's thinks. Oliver's thinks are Charles Dickens' thinks, and so are Nancy's. Charles Dickens' think is Fagin's, then it's mine, and now it's someone else's, on and on.

'Last night someone knocked Hart off his bike.' Quickly, the word went round. It was in the dark, and he got a hiding. Hart was on his way home from the Crown, and someone jumped out of the hedge. I imagined the exact place where it happened, and every thud of the punches, his tall old bike knocked sideways, and Hart falling into the bank at the roadside, and dragging himself the rest of the way to 'Staxford Villa'. It was the best thing we had heard for a very long time, perhaps the best ever. There was not overmuch talk of it, just a passing on of the good news. I think I know who did it, but shan't say.

CHAPTER 18

'Ought to be hoss-whipped', Grandma said. I interrupted a conversation as I opened the door into the living room from the passage-way. There was obvious embarrassment when I appeared, though, as the talk stopped immediately, I had no idea who was being discussed. But equally puzzling was Grandma saying 'hoss-whipped', like someone out of the Wild West rather than my grandmother.

Another time, Grandma stood with long skirts raised high and my mother was drawing Mrs Sturman's attention to how good the old lady's legs were still, beautifully smooth, and unmarked by years of having children, as I had heard Mum say before, because of her own varicose veins, in red lines on her lelegs. It was a moment cut short, as skirts dropped and a different conversation started up.

'I'll be on the warpath,' people said. 'If I hear of anyone doing that, I'll be on the warpath,' said Mrs Hart. 'If someone says that, I'll be on the warpath,' said Mum 'He's on the warpath'. 'You should hear her when she's on the warpath.' 'He's always on the warpath.' It was often being said. We got so used to it that it just seemed to mean being angry. But you could also think of Red Indians on their kind of warpath, moving quickly and silently into some place from which they could attack or defend. You could see them moving through bushes or among rocks, looking over a precipice, spying out the land, ready for action, and always silent, until the moment came, and all the cries.

'A bit of a grey wash there.' Mrs Sturman loved gossiping. One day, talking to my mother across the wire-netting fence, she looked further, to Aunt Ruth's linen line, or was it Aunt Dolly's on the other side?

I'm ten. I haven't drowned. Mum told me what the old woman said. She put her old head, her old black bonnet on, into my pram, and said, 'You'll never bring him up, my dear, that vein across his little nose, a sign he'll drown,' and Mum was scared. She was used to thinking what these old people said was often true, and anyway you couldn't forget what had been said however much you wanted to, and when Dad said, 'These bloody old wives' tales,' Mum said, 'but sometimes they come true, there's no denying that,' and Dad built a wooden thing on top of the old well, trying to make sure, but they never said I shouldn't fill the pail, just kept on saying, 'Be careful, John,' and I knew why it was, just couldn't stop from leaning over sometimes, looking down, you wouldn't see your face though, just a tiny shape of head a long way down, and skating on Rod Alley or the Ottermer, just, 'Careful, don't take risks because someone says do it, you've got more sense than that', and in the summer at Pakefield, she says ,'Now you'll be careful, I know that', and so I was, because mostly I was scared to go too far out like Russell did, but he could swim right out of his depth. I didn't even want to try. I haven't drowned, but 'you never know'. There's still a vein across my nose.

Mr Hart would not be headmaster of the new school that was being built behind Chattergate, somebody said, and somebody else said that was because of what he did that landed him in East Harling Court. We didn't know what he did, but nobody talked about it when children were near, because they were 'all ears'. It was something to do with things some of the girls in the 'big school' said about rudeness and things he said they should do. They didn't talk about it either, except probably among themselves. It was unbelievable that we should be free of him, so we also didn't talk of it. Mrs Sturman told Mum something about the trouble Hart was in. Hazel was one of the girls who had said things about him. We didn't know what they said because they didn't talk out, only among themselves. Someone said something about a girl being made to stand on the bench seat of a desk and lift her skirt up, but that didn't seem likely to be true. Hazel had taken me to the 'little school' on my first day, holding my hand, and I always liked her. She was visited every Sunday afternoon by her father, a thin, worried-looking man who came on a bike. We never knew why Hazel lived with Mrs Sturman, because our parents never told us. Perhaps they didn't know. But Mrs Sturman would have told my mother, because she liked to tell the things she knew. Somewhere around the time of the new school being built, Hazel left Mrs Sturman, but I didn't notice that she had gone until later. We were all so glad to escape from Hart.

One afternoon in the summer term of 1938, the new school was open to visitors. At the end of our school day, I went with Neville. We could walk from room to room, hardly believing how good it was. One room was especially good beyond all others. There was a teacher in there called Mr Witham. His room would be for crafts and science. He was to teach both subjects, and we knew from the moment he talked to us that we would love being with him for everything. We could hardly wait for Old Buckenham Area School to open.

A long time later, people said that Hart was no longer a teacher. He worked in an office in Norwich, something to do with the hiring out of boats on the river. The 'big school' stood empty, and however long anyone watched they would never see the top of Hart's bald head at his high windows. The bell would not sound again. Nobody would come running in fear of being late.

There was a missing uncle who was hardly ever mentioned. Among the ten children, Philip was next to Dad, about a year younger, the eighth. He had gone with Tom as a pupil to the City of Norwich School for Boys, at around the beginning of the Great War. What happened to Philip in 1914, when Tom had to leave school to become an engine driver, I never asked, and nobody ever thought to tell. What anyone who could be brought to mention him did say, was that it was a sad story that should not be talked about. The person who would talk was my mother. She had warm feelings towards Philip, and thought he had been badly treated when he got into trouble.

He liked alcohol too much, and wasted money. He forged his father's signature on cheques. Mum said there were stories of Philip being 'the worse for drink' in The Crown, a public house at the edge of the Green, which could be seen from Sunnyside. There were stories of banknotes falling from his pockets and Hart picking them up. Mum did not suggest that he was saving them for Philip. The point of her story seemed to be that there was never anything good to be said about Hart.

The outcome of the embarrassment Philip's behaviour caused his family was that, in his early twenties, he was found a job in Canada, in the corn trading business, and persuaded that his best opportunities would be there. His early letters home seemed to bear this out, but soon letters became fewer, and stranger. Then they stopped. His parents paid for phoney 'information' and 'investigation', but the story ended in silence and my grandmother's misery.

Uncle Oliver had gone to Canada several years earlier. He didn't talk of his own life. The telling came from my mother. After going to university, he went off to Canada to join the 'Mounties'. Soon, the Great War began, and Canada sent men to France. Uncle Oliver was among them.

Anyone whose story crossed the Atlantic became special to me. One of the men who came to live in a living van and to work with the threshing machines was Bert Allen. He had a very soft voice, and was a quiet, gentle man, probably not tough enough for the work of the threshing field. But Bert had been a lumberjack in Canada, and there were traces of Canada in his voice still. He seemed a man with sadness somewhere in his background, and hopes that he might never achieve. His great aim was to save enough money to buy a smallholding, so he could make a living by rearing animals.

Another man who had worked in North America was a farmer, the father of my friend Rex Taylor. Mr Taylor had actually been a cowboy, and brought back his truly huge broad-brimmed grey hat. It fell too low around my eyes and ears, but to be wearing it for a few moments was something I loved doing. Carr Farm, which was the first farm off the right-hand side of the Attleborough road, was a good place to be. The farmhouse was down a long driveway, so it was surrounded by the fields. One day Rex and I decided to make a tunnel into a strawstack. It was near another one, which partly hid us. The straw was clean and golden, and we pulled it out excitedly, thinking of how we would make a 'cave' in the middle, like those in the bushes 'down the holes'. But after a while of pulling out straw and passing it back to the outside, we lost our delight in the idea and gave up. Neither of us said anything about the danger we would have been in, and how two boys might have disappeared, and later been 'found smothered in the middle of a srawstack on Carr Farm'. We didn't need to say anything to each other. We pushed the straw back a bit to hide our foolishness, and went to do something else.

> Roll along covered wagon, roll along,
> To the turn of your wheels I sing a song.
> City ladies may be fine,
> But give me this gal of mine,
> Roll along covered wagon, roll along.

I sang that, and all the verses, over and over. You could feel you were the man at the reins, even if you were only ten. Going 'West' was a great adventure you could imagine too, putting together all the bits of what you knew from books and going to 'the pictures'. You're at the reins, two horses nodding heads, reins in both hands, between your fingers like they should be, nodding heads in rhythm, roll along, covered wagon, roll along, the iron wheel- rims grating on the rocks, or soft in grass, like all the way across the prairie, setting sun, and rising moon, and in the dark, and someone coming from the fire .and saying, 'Early start', and dreaming sitting there, the reins slap, slap across their backs, and feel the picking up of pace, the roll along, along, covered wagon, roll along, to the turn of your wheels, what song, what song, what girl? ...

Sliding on ice, on Rod Alley or Ottermer, was slide, slide, slide, slide, on and on and on, till you came to a standstill, or fell over when you tried to stop. Sliding on mud, was when you found a patch of short grass, slightly frosty, and you forced a slide on it, so the melting frost wetted the earth underneath, and the grass was slid away by feet following feet, until you had a long slide anyone might have thought impossible if they hadn't seen us do it. If it froze over in the night, there was a good ice slide in the morning.

There was a winter of deep snow, frozen hard by days and nights of the sharpest frosts. Dad had to move his threshing machinery from one farm to another, and the only way was through the main street of New Buckenham. Heavy iron clamps had to be bolted on to the great wheels of the engine, leaving a trail of rutted snow and angry people.

CHAPTER 19

Michael Faraday: my mother must have told me about him first, and second, third, and fourth, so that at last it was a something to be known and proud of, as I grew into whatever I was growing into, which was as hidden from me as was the future of those red squiggling larvae to themselves. Somewhere in my growing, I began to understand what baptism was, and that christening was another way of saying the same thing, and that one of the great scientists of Queen Victoria's time had baptised my grandfather. Grandad didn't talk of it, but he didn't need to, because of Mum's pleasure in telling things good to tell. But as I learnt more about Michael Faraday I realized that Mum's story was only the beginning.

There had been a tiny chapel behind Rod Alley Row. People who went there were

Sandemanians. My great-grandfather's brother, Thomas Elisha, was one of them, and on a few days in 1860 Michael Faraday, who was an Elder of the Sandemanian Church, was his guest. It was then he baptized the baby who would grow up to be my grandfather.

I was lucky that he was able to be my grandfather. There was a story that was told by other people, but he never talked about. When he was about forty years old, a steam engine that he was driving exploded. A man who was working with him was killed.. Grandad was scalded all over and had a broken leg. He was in a coma for many days. When he recovered, he invented a safety valve that could be fitted on the top of an engine, with a whistle to warn of danger. In school we learned that James Watt said, 'Necessity is the Mother of Invention'. He was an engine driver too.

It was best when people talked about nowadays.

'Her lips are always set so tight you wouldn't be able to get a razor blade between them.'

If you listened to Mr Bush talking, he was always likely to say something that made you want to go on listening. Another thing about his talking was that he easily included the children as his listeners, where most adult visitors seemed to ignore us. We always liked 'Bush' to come tapping on the inner door from

175

the hallway, often around bedtime, which was a good reason to stay quiet and listen. There was always something odd and funny about the way he said things. He also looked odd and funny. His face was very much alive when he sat there with a chair pulled up to the table, his big nose poking out, his eyes full of something like mischief, enjoying having his listeners.

When he said about a razor blade, I wondered who the lady was.

At weekends, I was 'Little John'. John Hart, who came with his mother to stay with Uncle Harry and Aunt Gee, was 'Big John'. His Hart name came from his father being brother to my headmaster. Aunt Ada seemed to be pleased that her son was given, somehow, more importance by her way of naming us. She was the only person who actually said Big John and Little John, but I knew that everyone accepted the rightness of her idea simply because she was a bossy person who expected obedience. She was a headmistress at the school in Deopham, a few miles away, beyond Attleborough.

John was about two years older than me, so he was bigger anyway. We said we were cousins, but actually it was my father and Aunt Ada who were cousins, making us half cousins, which always seemed less important. John had a bad leg. The bone was diseased, and from time to time it got worse. For several weeks on end he had to stay in bed. As a result of his illness, one leg was shorter. It didn't show when he walked because the sole on one shoe was much higher than the other. Sometimes Aunt Ada gave my mother his 'left offs', clothes or shoes. Once, when I had to take the shoes to Mr Kettle for altering, he said, 'Ah, you've had these from the other John!'

Big John was a good friend. I always looked forward to the weekends, and always wandered about sadly after he went home on Sunday afternoons. We usually sat together in Uncle Harry's pew in church, so most of our good times came on Saturdays. He went to a posh school in Norwich, Unthank College, but never acted posh in spite of that.

Aunt Ada came to say something to us.

'There's a little word I do not like, and wish not to hear' She didn't wish to say it either, so she spelt it out. 'Ess-oh-dee. I do *not* expect to hear it again.'

To be 'Little John' gave me a reminder of Robin Hood and Sherwood Forest, but it also stayed the way Aunt Ada puffed herself up with pride.

The saddest part of the Robin Hood story was when Robin told his friends that he would shoot an arrow and where it struck would be the place they should bury him. It fell under the greenwood tree he had chosen. When I saw the arrow in my mind, it was not in Sherwood Forest but under a big ash on Old Buckenham Green A moment later it was in the Sherwood I imagined.

One day at Pakefield, Olive cried. The hamster lay dead in a little cardboard box. She took me up the garden, showed me where to bury him. We covered him with earth. It was a something needed, something done. Tomorrow she would remember, but smile again. I would too.

King George V was dead. The man on the wireless had said, 'The life of the King is drawing slowly to its close ...' Now, Dad had his head behind his *Sunday Express*. He was reading something about the new king, Edward the Eighth, who had not yet had his coronation, deciding he would rather marry his American lady-friend, Mrs Simpson, than be crowned King of England without her as his Queen. Dad was saying things to Mum about it. Suddenly, he was angry. He *exclaimed,* as people do in books.

'Bloody old whore.'

Mum exclaimed too.

'Oh, Tom.'

It was a word I did know about for sure. I thought about hips and haws. Haws are the little dark red berries of the hawthorn. Hips are the larger, light red berries of the wild rose, so you see them together in hedges. I found out about Dad's word quite soon afterwards.

An old man stood at his gate, next to the yard at Chattergate, as we passed when going along that side of the Green. There had been two brothers, but one was dead. The cottage faced south, so the old man could stand in the sun. He always wore his old cap and his old-fashioned suit. His name was Mr Frost, and we always spoke a greeting. I couldn't remember noticing when he was no longer there. That seems a sad thing.

Dan Brown came to Rod Alley quite often at weekends, red-faced and friendly, a butcher from Pulham. He was Aunt Dolly's brother. One trip was different and special. He took Dad and Uncle Dick to Ipswich for a boxing show. It was a men's outing, but I felt envious, as if I might have expected to be included. I was beginning to know about boxing, and had followed the name of Frank Hough, who was top of the bill. I don't know why this occasion should seem so special, but it did.

Old Henry Anderson, the vicar, peered through little gold-rimmed spectacles with pale and watery eyes. He had written on small sheets of paper he could hold in one hand easily, so he could look at us as he talked to us in Sunday school. It seemed as if he always wanted to be sure that what he said was exactly as he wrote it out. He must have been forgetful. He was very old. His handwriting was strange and beautiful. It was not quite joined up, more like the print in beautiful old books, the kind monks worked on all their lives. On Sunday mornings he taught us in Hart's classroom, from ten o'clock until half-past. I had just time to get home and go on to Uncle Harry's house, to walk across the green with his family to church, which was from eleven o'clock till twelve. In the afternoon, I had to be back in church by two, for Sunday school again, old Henry Anderson and his beautiful handwriting. He would stand among us, down in the aisle, our pews on either side, his script in his left hand, his right hand grasping on the high carved decoration of a pew. The old man must have been quite tired. There was still Evensong a few hours on. He must have been grateful for the lovely writing he held close and high. We didn't understand a lot of what he said. He didn't know that, because he never asked us questions, just talked on. He did the writing years before.

One Christmas at Sunnyside, one of the visiting aunts brought table fireworks, and after tea the big table was cleared for strange curling 'snakes' of greyish colour to come magically out of lighted cones, to slide across the trays, sputtering and curling, and seem half-funny, half quite horrible, but harmless-if-you're-sensible, surprising shapes making aunts get over-excited and making your eyes as big-as-could-be if you could have seen them in a looking-glass. It happened other years, but it was just once for me because I happened to be there.

'Big John' got his bad leg again, much worse than it had ever been before. He couldn't come to stay with Uncle Harry and Aunt Gee at the weekends. Mum said I should let him have my model steam engine that Grandad had given me, so he had it to play with in his bedroom while he was having to stay in bed. And I was able to imagine him having the engine puffing away on a little table at his bedside, the piston speeding in and out so fast you could hardly see it, and the flywheel spinning so fast you couldn't see the spokes, and John being happy, lying there, propped up a bit with pillows so he could watch, and listen to the chuff and whirr, and think of me, and of being at Old Buck when he was well again.

But it was a long, long time before he came again. I didn't know how exactly long it was, but it was long enough to make me to long for it to be how it had been before, even if there had to be the boring time in church, the prayers, the leaning forward pretending that your knees were on the hassock thing (like some, both men's and ladies', really were), and all the things we had to answer-back when the

Reverend Henry Anderson asked us to, the long, long hymns, the Holy, Holy, Holy words, the organ noises Mr Bush was good at, really loud, or sometimes little squeaky bits between, and psalms of David, at the lectern, then the high-up-there-in-the-pulpit parson with his little piece of paper in his hand, until it ended and the poor old man came down, then one more hymn that Mr Bush could hurry us through, and Uncle Harry coming round with that little dark red bag that hung therte for our coins, and we were filing out into the sun or wind or rain.

And never again did I see my engine, though Dad 'got on' at Mum for 'giving it to Ada' and not asking for it back, though John was better and he came for weekends every Saturday again, and somehow it happened that I never asked him why he didn't bring my engine with him, as if he thought that having it a while had made it his. And when Dad 'got on' at Mum, I wondered why he never asked Aunt Ada for himself – she was his cousin, so it would have been quite easy for him, anyway. So many things are puzzling. Then we forget them, till they puzzle us again. 'Once in a while', you think. You love those words. 'Once in a while': Grandad's engine was just that, but somehow more.

Near the way into the orchard at Sunnyside, on the far side from the house, and near Grandad's garage, there was a very old brick building. It was quite small, with a low roof, and you could see the undersides of the rooftiles through the rafters. I went in there alone and looked at the thing Dad had shown me quite a long time ago. Now, I was tall enough to reach it by standing on something. It was the slightly-curved scabbard of a sword, very rusty, with a dull red rust and grey flecks mottled over it. At the top end, was a rusty spike that had fixed the missing handle. Dad had told me it was from the 'Crinean War', and had been used by his Great-Uncle Birt, whose name was spelt like that because it was a surname on Grandma's side of the family. And Dad's middle name was Birt too, in memory of the soldier.

I knew I could reach the sword, so I did, and carefully took it down. It was quite heavy, and the spike felt strange to hold. I wondered where the handle had gone. The curve of the scabbard was slight. When I pulled , the blade was a bit tight, then slid smoothly out. I stood looking down at it, not gleaming now, but still a sword that had been in battles, and slashed at many soldier's bodies in 1854. I held it a while, and turned it about to feel its weight, then slid it back. Outside, the sun was bright, and it was the twentieth century, and for tea Aunt Violet might have made some Bakewell tarts..

Harry Ayton did his 'paper round' by horse and cart. Sometimes, he brought his wife. He came down Rod Alley from the White Horse end. We had the *Daily Express*. I read it a bit, murders, the war in Abyssinia, looked at cartoons, but went to the Rupert stories and their illustrations first. Many people took the 'E D P', the *Eastern Daily Press*. Most of the papers were *Daily* Something: *Herald, Mail, Mirror,* or *Telegraph*. Harry never looked at lists to see which paper went wherever, nor at records of who-owed-what. He was as regular as the postman was in where you'd see him on the roads. His only delays were on the journey home. His little horse stood patiently, sometimes outside the Sun or the Crown, but, always, the White Horse, grazing or with a nosebag.

Harry was a well-liked little man, cheery, peak-capped. He didn't seem to notice children though. His wife was busy-looking, with dark eyes, a touch of gipsy in them. One thing, I think, made me 'think twice', as my mother would have put it, was that he would take horses for the knacker's yard, which was where they were slaughtered, to be cut up in little pieces as pet food for dogs and cats, or fed in big pieces to animals in zoos. That makes a picture now, the horse and cart off into the distance on the Attleborough road, some old, unwanted nag, haltered, following.

CHAPTER 20

Partway along the path from our back gate (and Uncle Leslie's), at a place opposite the greengage tree and an old Great War railway horsebox, which was now used for storing sacks, there was a low storage place for planks. It was covered by sheets of corrugated iron. On one of these, there appeared one of my grandfather's bowler hats. When it remained there for a few days, I started to use it as a target for my airgun. Lead pellets pattered into it. Small darts with red or blue plumes could be collected and fired again. The touch of realism given by this unusual target did not bother me, and nobody said any disapproving word.

The horsebox was a railway thing, a great wooden box on iron wheels, big enough to hold, perhaps, six horses in, all bound for France in Great War days. Few horses ever came back fit for anything. Most died as soldiers did. I didn't know how or when it came to be there in the yard. Grandad had sacks of grain in store, perhaps. Now, empty sacks were piled, just thrown in anyhow. We played in there, or sat and talked. Some boards had parted slightly, so light came in.

A lady whose husband died was called a 'widow woman', but the way we said it was more like 'widder woman'. There were many of them after the Great War. For people of my age, so many years had passed, we didn't always know why someone lived alone, unless we heard our mothers use the words 'widder woman'. Then we thought a bit, but not for long, because 'they're young' and 'they don't realize'.

A gateway into a walled garden was to the right of Grandad's garage at Sunnyside. The garden was kept tidy by Aunt Violet, but otherwise nobody ever seemed to go there. There was a flower, a peony, dark red and leafy, that I thought was the most beautiful flower I had ever seen. It was Aunt Violet who told me its name. I thought of a story in one of my annuals, in which a very old man watched some children as they played. When I turned to the page in the book, a picture of the old man, a simple black-and-white drawing, filled me with fear. He was in the walled garden. The cause of the fear was that the children in the story did not know he was watching them. Regardless of the events of the story, he seemed a threat to them, and a threat to me.

You never forget the look of new and perfect chickens' eggs in their nests, nor the smoothness and warmth of their shells. Nor the way they can be each of a slightly different shade from mid-pinky-brown to white, and how they are of the same shade all over. And you never forget gathering them for the first time in a basket and taking them back to the house. And you know that other people are having the same feelings every day. Even the shape of the golden straw nest is perfect, from the shape of the hen's body, pressing down, so the eggs stay close and can't roll away.

Aunt Violet showed me how to gather them carefully and take them in through the scullery door at Sunnyside. Before the door, was a space covered in like a greenhouse with glass. In the afternoon and evening, the sunlight came through.

Nearly all my times with Aunt Violet were at Sunnyside, then one was very different. She was on her bicycle. It was the first time we had ridden bikes together, so there was a special feeling for this outing to 'the pictures' in Attleborough. She had asked if I would like to come with her but it felt that she had come with me. The picture was called 'The Lost Horizon'.

Ronald Colman was the star, handsome, with his black moustache, the story from a book Aunt Violet must have read. An airplane crashed in a Tibetan valley, Shangri-la, a wonderland, a place whose peoples seemed not to grow old. But, after a while, the visitors longed to know their own lost world again. They slipped away, to travel through the mountain fastness. A girl of Shangri-la, in love with Colman's brother, travelled too, fell ill. When they tried to care for her, uncovering her face, what they saw was not the beauty but a hideous old woman. Here was what she had become outside her valley, all the unchanging so undone. The moment made us gasp, cry out in horror, in the little picture house, as if we too were travelling from Shangri-la.

There was an argument one day, when we played cricket on the Green, about the best position for a batsman to take when facing a bowler. What we thought and said, shouting our certainties depended on which photograph we had studied of Don Bradman. Some showed him standing upright, bat near his boots, some, with left knee bent, right leg stretched backwards. The ball, of course, was out of the picture. Our certainties depended on whether we knew which picture was *before*, which *after*, but we could stay certain in lovely ignorance or go home afterwards and eat our tea in more accurate knowledge, and think how we were living in the time of Don Bradman.

Rabbits would always be there on the road, somewhere near Bungay. Whenever we travelled home at night from Pakefield, there would be one that stayed when all the others leapt aside. It would bound ahead, so terrified, right at the centre of the road, as if the light on either side was what they had to fear. They didn't dare to cross towards the dark beyond the two light beams, only to try to reach the dark ahead, that didn't come near however hard they ran. But always, in the end, as Dad slowed more, there would be a sideways leap into the dark and safety there. A short way on, there'd be another group, the same thing happening. Perhaps the ones who leapt sideways straightaway were those who'd learned. The ones who ran were young and ignorant.

The boy stood alone. The others in the drawing in the book were a group that looked towards him, saying something to each other, as such groups do, of what they thought of him. It was a drawing in a book for boys, and girls perhaps, but mostly boys, about this boy who at that moment stood apart. He was Napoleon. This was France, and they were French. He was Corsican. Corsica was an island ruled by France. It was not far off, but it was not France. It had been ruled by Italy. It was not a place to come from if you didn't want to stand alone in the garden of the military school these boys were in. The little drawing said so much. I sat and looked at it, and read the words. And every time the book was read, I looked at the drawing yet again.

There were strange words I liked to look at, say, and feel their sound. 'Magyar' was on stamps, Hungarian. 'Mag-yar': you didn't need to know a meaning. It was the sound, and feelings that came and you couldn't call by any name.

Someone 'went gallivanting about', Mum would say, and you wouldn't quite know what 'gallivanting' was. It wasn't just going somewhere in any ordinary way. Then you noticed that people who gallivanted were somehow a bit like each other. It could be 'show-offs', or people who got noticed for the clothes they wore, or people who could just please themselves about what they did. Then you found it said about yourself or one of our friends, and you knew she was just being amusing by making them like a really gallivanting person. I went 'gallivanting off somewhere' when she didn't know where I was going.

Another thing she talked about was someone being 'squeamish', and I already knew what it meant. But she said it wrongly. She said 'screamish', and didn't seem to know that it was wrong. I thought that was because it was about things that might make anyone feel like screaming. I didn't tell her it was wrong.

Iris Williamson stood with us and talked. She liked to have us stand close and talk about something. You listened and liked her to notice you as she talked, or notice you specially when you said something when she asked you a question or told you something when you asker her. She was a bit older than us. I couldn't remember her at either the little school or Hart's school, and didn't know if she had been at either. Now she was at 'Thetford Grammar' and was proud of that. She liked to stand with 'good posture' always, knowing she looked good, and that we knew she looked good. You noticed her high little bosom, and she liked it and knew how you felt. And she enjoyed that because she knew it was part of the reason for being there, listening and looking and wanting to stay. And we were kind of grateful for her bothering to be with us, taking notice when we spoke, which we didn't do much, and we were always disappointed when she turned away.

We had a different car, a Triumph Dad had bought from Uncle Percy. A cloudburst came. Dad stopped the car, put off the windscreen wiper, let the rain do what it would.

'Cloudburst. We'll sit and wait.'

It slashed against the windscreen, white, and blocking out the sight of anything outside. The side windows too showed nothing but the rain, in streams, in slashes, lessening a moment, slashing again, squalling suddenly to blind us more, the drumming roof, the sound of cudgelling almost, then suddenly, a cease, the unbelieving looking out, in front, and all around, the sky, a dark wood is on one side, a field the other, in front the bending road, a gleam of sun, the rain still falling. Dad tried to start the car. There was the sound I'd heard before, a gasping, losing sound, but then the engine came alive.

'Look out for the rainbow,' Mum said. 'Look, there it is.'

CHAPTER 21

There was a small greyhound track at Bunwell, a few miles away, on the Norwich road, beyond New Buckenham. Uncle Dick went there regularly and sometimes took me. One of the good things about going with Uncle Dick in his van was that he liked to let me hold the steering wheel, with his own hands ready to prevent accidents. There was very little traffic, and he knew we were safe. One dog he liked to put in races was called Jean. Her racing name was Buckenham Lady. Jean didn't win, but the thrill was in the racing, with about half-a-dozen dogs yelping with excitement before the start, then tearing after the electric hare as it whirred round the track, well ahead at the start, then just about to be caught before it stopped, when the dogs once again jumped around, now in disappointment. They knew, mostly, that it was a fake, but they liked to believe, just for a few moments that, this time, it was real. No dog ever failed to run. Oh, the lovely mad things. They never seemed to feel cheated. A dog might run several times in an evening, as keen in the last race as in the first.

Our chasing after a football was similar. First, we picked captains, though usually they had already picked themselves. Sometimes they just said it. 'I'll be captain,' and we pretended our happy agreement. It was easier that way, and dusk was falling so we needed to get started.

We stood in a line and the captains picked us.

'My first pick,' one would usually say, and the other agreed, because that was easier and he never wanted the boy that Billy picked anyway.

After they picked us, we lined up behind them, always knowing who should be last. But sometimes it happened the usual last hadn't come to play, had the bellyache, or was looking after his little sister, and someone else stood not wanting to be the one not chosen, the one left over, who never got in the line with the captains because already the rest were piling their goalpost jackets and spreading for 'centre'

Then, even the last-chosen would chase like mad for a miracle goal and their wild admiration, though soon the ball was getting greasy in the dew-sodden grass, and skidded away off your boot in the wrong direction, and the other side took it and easily scored, and everyone shouted you'd kicked the wrong way.

It was a time of changes. 'The electric' came, and all the old oil lamps that had made it just about possible to see each other as we drew close to the table, faces against the dark, were put away or thrown out. Then came the running water, with splashing taps, old wells no longer needed, the squeaking kitchen pumps with their long, curved handles now idle. And the new school was being built, just past Chattergate, with almost everyone, perhaps, expecting children suddenly to show how brainy they really were.

The ancient willow trunk had been taken away. Soon it was replaced by a bright red telephone kiosk. 'Kiosk' was a word we had not heard till then. Mrs Sturman said it was a 'ky-orsk'.

Amelia Earhart, the daring flyer, disappeared on a flight round the world which would have been the first ever. Below, was the Pacific, all the way to homeland America. Never to arrive, never fly out of clear blue to a happy landing. To lie somewhere and never be found. So that someone will say, 'I wonder what happened to Amelia Earhart?', and imagine the Electra dropping out of the sky, to the jungle or ocean, parting of waves and the closing over, as if she had never been there. But there she was, and will be while we remember, a face behind goggles, a helmeted head, a speck going down to the hazy horizon.

Aunt Allie (she was my mother's aunt) kept a pub, The Star, with Uncle Jack Hancey, at the market place in Diss, which was about nine miles from Old Buckenham. There was a covered yard behind, where market men could leave their horse and cart. It smelt of horse piss, on Fridays especially. At the bottom end, there was a doorway to the mere, with hens and ducks around an uncovered yard down to the lapping water, where the ducks slipped in and sped about, or sat among the ripples, and quacked when we appeared.

Uncle Jack looked like a man who ran a pub. He was quite short, a little stout, red faced, grey haired, with joking eyes. Aunt Allie was taller, paler, more serious, but just as welcoming. She always dressed in black.

'Would you like a shortcake, John?' Aunt Allie brought a big round tin. The lid was off. The cakes were big and square, twice as thick as any ever seen. I took the nearest one, like Mum had said you always should. 'I think you like shortcakes,' Aunt Allie said. I was already biting it. 'Don't speak with your mouth full,' Mum always said. The cake was heavy, moist. I hadn't lied.

The Friday bar was full of happy-sounding, know-all men, who drank and slapped their pots down for 'Another, if you please, ma'am', and steadily got louder, till they remembered market stall, or shop, or horse, or wife, and went outside.

There was a very thin small man who lived at the Star as a lodger. Everyone liked him and called him 'Old Bob'. He always wore an old cap with a big peak. I never saw him without it. He could even have worn it in bed. He had been a soldier in the Great War.

Aunt Allie liked to ride with William Whitehand in his pony trap when they were young. He was a good-looking young fellow, and liked making a show for her because she was an attractive girl. One day they were passing young women by the roadside, perhaps going to or coming from church, as it was a Sunday, and William started singing to them about themselves, 'I'm Seventeen, Come Sunday', a popular song of those times. The memory of it was with her all her life, of a happy young man who had a sad life ahead of him. One thing people noticed about Aunt Allie was that when she told a story, she could usually tell the exact date it happened. Whether the dates were true, nobody knew.

CHAPTER 22

A knock at the door. My mother said, 'See who it is.' I went to see, opened the door to nobody there. The hall was dim, outside was dark, but there was a parcel on the step. Just as my fingers touched, it moved, a rolled-up package slipped away a foot or two, and when I stepped out, and bent again, it jerked. I guessed a string, a 'someone' in the dark, outside the gate. After a few steps more, it stayed. I picked it up, pulled in the string. When I went in, to the lamp-lit table with my sisters round, brown paper part unrolled, the string untied, there was a call of 'Er-r' as a big pink pig's ear fell out, and Mum just said, 'That's Uncle Dick.' The day was St Valentine's, not long before the war.

Uncle Leslie had tried that kind of trick. I think it was the year before. He had knocked on the scullery door. I lifted the latch. As the door came open, our bristly yard broom fell on me. It wasn't quite as good a trick as Uncle Dick's surprise.

Edgar Sparrow had a little bicycle shop, next to his old flint-stone house, between that and the corner garage Uncle Dick hired to put his van in, but never did. The shop was so small it was not much more than a shed, with only space enough for a narrow counter, old Edgar behind, a customer in front. We brought our bike with punctures, or came for valve- rubber to fix. Valve rubber cost a 'ha'penny', he mended a puncture for a penny. His prices were too small, and everyone said that. But Edgar was so honest he would hate to charge too much. Not really 'hate'. Old Edgar was a man who wouldn't hate. He was just good. 'A good old man,' they said. If I tried to think of a good man, I'd think of Edgar. His shop was only opened when a customer came, and even then it was only if he was not too busy in his blacksmith's place. You had to choose your time right, and he'd come. He used to take your photographs, a long time ago, when only a few people would have a camera. Some people said he was Edgar Punt. Perhaps Punt was his mother's name.

On Sundays for chapel, Edgar looked really smart. He had his suit and new cap on. It had been his new cap many years. The cap he wore for work had been his old cap for very much longer, blackened by smoke from his workshop furnace and touches from his hard-working hands.

A pine wood separated Uncle Dick's piece of land, 'the rough', as he called it, from the grounds of the Hall, the grandest building in the village. We became used to going to the Hall grounds during a time when the building stood empty after the last of its grand owners left. There was a thrill to coming out of the darkness of the pines to a wide expanse of water, a lake that had been created in the little river. We liked to know that we were trespassing. It was especially good to trespass here now, because we knew we wouldn't be caught.

One day, I came there with Alan Gedge. We found a boat in a boathouse and tried a lock and chain because it looked an easy job to pull them from the wall and take the boat. Soon we were using the punting poles to glide out from the edges to the clear water circling an island. Not all of the water was clear. Weeds grew thickly in places, so we had to find our way carefully for some distance before we could draw up to the island, where we felt as if we had achieved something, though in fact the island was small and held no great interest.

Our trouble started on the way back. The weeds were more difficult to move through as we became more confident and less careful. The punt poles needed more expert hands and were in danger of sticking in mud and being separated from us. When Alan was in the rear, taking his turn at punting, we moved to suddenly clear water. The boat shot forward, and I was watching Alan clinging to his upright pole, which then slowly tilted and lowered him to the water. He struggled in the weeds, shouting to me for help. I punted back and helped him over the side, and we decided to get to shore.

Alan undressed and beat his clothes hard against a tree, first trousers, next shirt, then trousers again. His underpants and vest had to be twisted tightly, and trousers slapped against the tree a few more times. As he dressed he was more concerned about what his mother would say than about the uncomfortable walk home. His punting days, and mine, were over.

Uncle Dick was angry. He had found a boy on his land, 'the rough'. The greyhounds were yelping for their food.

'You dirty little bugger', he said to Wilfred. 'Done your jobs in the trench I dug.'

'I didn't.'

'It was you.'

'When?'

'You know when'.

'No.'

'*Someone* did it. Yesterday.'

Wilfred saw his chance.

'Was it cobbly?'

'You know it was.'

'It was Denny Large, then,' said Wilfred. 'That's who it would be. I wasn't here yesterday.'

'You're here t'day,' Uncle Dick said. 'What's that for?'

'Just saw your dogs.' Anyone knew that mention of dogs would change Uncle Dick's mood.

We loved trespassing, whether it was on Bush's farm, to the ice-hill, on that other farm for peas in the pod, in the old deserted garden of the empty Whitehand house at Stacksford, in the pine wood behind Uncle Dick's place called 'the rough', in the boathouse at the Hall, or on the lake there and its island, or through any gap in a hedge that let us into a field or meadow for a bird's-nest or blackberries, or simply because the gap was there, or just any place we thought someone would think we shouldn't be in, would give us that strange thrill, a bit of excitement, a bit of fear, the feel of being daring or outwitting someone (even if we didn't know who it was) – or even just thinking the word itself, 'tres-pass-ing'—gave us something we had to do, only because it was possible, and we wanted to do it without being caught. But we couldn't help wondering why the prayer we said at school and church and Cawston's Meeting had to use that same word, for something else.

Saw-bench time was mostly in the summer, early, before harvest and the threshing season. You could always tell when it started, by the quick blade's scream from the foundry yard, usually at the wide piece of ground near the orchard. You rushed to see, and there was Dad, guiding a tree trunk towards the big circular saw-blade, whirring in its place on the bench, only its top half showing above the saw-bench, as it tore through the wood, with sawdust thrown all around in a cloud. The way the wood moved forward was on a trolley that supported the weight, running on iron rails set in two long, very solid, lengths of wood, about a yard apart. There would be a man or two men, pushing. Dad would be near the saw, guiding. The power for the saw would come through a driving-belt connected to a quite small stationary engine, petrol-driven, beyond the far end of the bench.

When the trunk had travelled through, its whole length divided by the blade, the trolley supporting it would be pulled back, ready for another journey, another long scream. This would leave a gleaming white plank of poplar or elm or ash, ready to be lifted away, later to be dried under the long, wide area of corrugated-iron roof we called the woodshed, which was where it might stay for years, seasoning, with small dividing strips between the planks, so air could circulate. You loved to sit there in the scent of wood, hidden away where nobody knew.

For later sawing of planks, there was another saw-bench, smaller. It was driven by the old Peugeot car with all its covering parts stripped off, so only the chassis and engine remained. The Peugeot was in a shed built on a corner of the foundry, and the driving-belt connected to a small saw-bench standing outside .

I sometimes looked in to see the old car standing there in the shadows. Nobody but myself was in the whole of the foundry and workshop building. There was a feeling of past things and past times.

I didn't know how to pronounce the name 'Peugeot'. We said, 'Pewjo'.

Just inside the foundry yard from the corrugated iron gate to the Green, there was a recess between walls of the workshop wide enough and deep enough for couple of small elder trees to grow among a scatter of rusted iron pieces and nettles. In front of them was a water butt, low but wide, part of the barrel of an ancient steam engine, perhaps old enough to be from one of the first engines ever made. It must have been used as a water butt for many years. I could not remember when it was not there. The engine it came from must have been very old indeed to have been broken up.

The water came in from iron roof-guttering, and quickly turned greenish, with a rusty colour around the edge. Red, squiggling larvae gleamed near the surface. Tap the rim, and they scuttled down instantly, stayed out of sight for a few moments, wriggled up and hung at the surface. Tap again, and they were gone. They did not learn however many times you tapped. I did not wonder if they had to come up for breath. I did not know what they turned into, and never asked anyone and nobody told me. It would have been something that flew away.

CHAPTER 23

After the pine wood, Neville and I stood watching to see if we were likely to be able to venture further round the lake at the Hall. It was months after the visit with Alan Gedge that had ended with his lowering into the water on a punting pole. Now, the reason for our hesitation was that the Hall was no longer unoccupied. Boys from the posh private school moved in small groups in the distance. We had become used to going to the Hall grounds. Now, we felt resentful of these newcomers. They, rather than ourselves, seemed like the intruders, taking our place of adventure. There was no chance of a friendly meeting, as we knew by instinct. We also knew that after walking the distance from the village we were not ready to turn homeward. Perhaps we sensed we were ready for whatever might happen if the new lot saw us. One thing giving us confidence was that the flow of water from the lake into the stream would separate the Hall boys from us, however near they came. The lake water ran over a brick ridge and down a slope of small cobblestones into the little river. A few boys became aware of us. They stopped moving, probably to decide what to do, then came forward warily. Soon, they were facing us across the watery slope.

'Clear orf.'

'You can't come here.'

'Who says?'

'We do'. Several said it.

'Who are you to say we can't?'

'You don't belong here.'

'Who says?' The 'orf' sounded posh. Enough to make us ready to enjoy the daring we were beginning to feel. 'Clear orf, clear orf.' We mimicked. 'Clear orf y'self.'

We enjoyed standing up to the strangers. They became ready enemies. They looked down on us as village boys. We were half amused by their 'la-di-dah' voices, half sorry for them because of the way they all had to look alike when they walked in their long ranks to church, grey suits and ringed caps in light and dark blue.

So the words built up, 'clever dick' words from them, jeering from us. Then I felt a grip on one of my shoulders, and Neville felt a grip on one of his. The schoolboys had gone silent, and we had not noticed because of our own jeers.

'And – who – are – you?'

Mr Sewell, headmaster of the boarding-school, turned us to face him by the strength of his grip. Among the boys there was some murmuring and tittering. I wondered how they had managed to watch him come close without letting us see we were about to be caught. I realized that a couple had sneaked away to bring him round the edge of the lake.

'Your names?' he said

Weakly, one of us was Robinson, the other, Jones. My mind leapt to Sunday, when old Sewell would be able to look across in church and see me in Uncle Harry's pew. He told us off, said he didn't want ever to see us by the lake again, and gave us each a push. Then he walked away along the path he had come by.

The boys from Old Buckenham Hall were led each Sunday by their teachers in a column to church. It was a longish walk, and they probably straggled somewhat, but when they emerged on the Banham Road they had to look impressive, in their caps with rings of two shades of blue, advancing towards the crossing of the Council Road, then down the sloping road to Church Lane. In church they sat in the part between the lectern and the altar, sideways-on to the rest of the congregation, under the great stained-glass window with the huge figure of the bearded old man I always thought might be God. In this position, with only a few of the village people who chose to have their private pews in that part of the church, they could survey the rest of us. Perhaps they made a kind of choir, adding more to the singing than all the others. Somewhere behind, on the left, was Mr Bush at the organ, usually seeming to be playing something to please himself, complicated, grand, something the rest could either put up with or admire. One of the parishioners on the right, in his private pew, was Mr Mawby. He was one of Grandad's customers. Grandad was always sure to talk to his customers politely. He said that was the correct thing to do in 'business'. Mr Mawby was never simply 'Mawby', always 'Mr Mawby'. Dad sometimes said, 'Bloody old Mawby'

... 'A bit of jiggery-pokery,' Mum said. She said it quite often. It meant that there was something to be suspicious about in what someone had said or done. She liked people who were plainly honest, people who showed their intentions. Most people were like that, but some, especially some in newspapers, were 'up to a bit of jiggery-pokery'. You wondered what it was, and if they would be 'found out'.

Another saying like that, was, 'Well, I'll be jiggered'. It meant someone was very surprised or couldn't believe.

'What do you want to do when you're grown up, John?' Aunt Hilda asked. She said it as 'want to <u>doo</u>'. It was posh'

'A journalist.' Saying it made me feel timid.

'Oh, I'm afraid you'll find that won't be within your reach.' She sounded sorry, but snooty at the same time. 'You're at an elementary school, and a journalist needs grammar school.'

She seemed to know. She smiled kindly, with a thin little mouth and pale blue eyes. There were tiny freckles all over her face. She lived at Stourbridge, which was a posh place near Birmingham. I think she said 'Stooerbridge', which made it sound posher still. Birmingham wasn't a posh place, but was the 'second city' of England, Mrs Hart had said.

I didn't stop wanting to be a journalist.

CHAPTER 24

Iturned to look behind me, away from the dinner table. Aunt Stella was sitting in an armchair, giving a breast to her baby. The breast was big, with light blue veins. The brown nipple was wet. The baby was about to go back on it. I was glad, glad, glad to have seen something so good to see, if only for a moment

When Uncle Percy and Aunt Stella came to stay for a few days , the table had to be made bigger so we could all sit round it. This was done by putting in another 'leaf' which was an extra piece of the table that would appear between the two other 'leaves' when they were moved apart by turning a little iron handle. Mum would always have to call my sisters and my cousin Margaret from wherever they happened to be, because it was usual for them to be wherever Thora had led the younger ones off to as soon as the visitors arrived, in the garden, the orchard, or another room. Barbara and Margaret had been born on the same day. Thora, as she was two years older, liked to feel she was in charge.

'There!' Uncle Dick lets Jean go free from the lead. She leaps forward , bounding to a pattern like down, down, up...down, down, up, which is like the movement of the hare. They go through the stubble and grass, then up and over, up and over, the hare a poor desperate thing, the dog mad with excitement and instinct to kill. But when the edge of the field is reached, there is a way through the hedge for the hare but not for the dog, and Uncle Dick hurries forward, calling her to come to him She enjoys his praise, whimpering and nuzzling as he puts on the lead, and he is happy, knowing that I have seen something for the first time, glad to have shown me. We go on a bit but know we shall not find another hare, because every wild thing will be scared and crouching away from danger. I am glad the hare got away, but would not say that to Uncle Dick.

Somewhere in the early weeks of the new school, I began to notice a girl among a group from New Buckenham, and I thought she was noticing me. I walked along their way as they biked up Abbey Road from Chattergate. One day she seemed interested enough to separate from the rest, with a friend, as if ready for me to say something. I don't know what I said, but she stopped, and the friend stopped too.

She had a round, full face, pretty and smiling. We talked in a hesitant, embarrassed way, for the rest of Abbey Road, to the corner opposite Rod Alley. Then she said to the friend that perhaps they should hurry on now. We said 'See you tomorrow', and they pedalled away, looking back a bit.

The next afternoon, I waited for her a short way from Durrants', tiny shop opposite Chattergate, with a bar of Milky Way. She was happy to stop again, but this time the friend went on slowly, waiting, leaving Gabrielle to have her time with me. So started a pattern of pleasure and exploring. Sometimes we were together well past the Rod Alley corner, and her friend went ahead of us up the Green.

Gabrielle said her surname was Kidd and that she really came from somewhere away and lived with her aunt in New Buckenham. I wondered why she didn't live with her parents, but didn't ask her. When she raced on to catch up with her friend, she looked back and put up a hand.

With Mrs Twiddy, we read *King Solomon's Mines* by Rider Haggard, who was a Norfolk man in Queen Victoria's time. I had noticed that a book could be 'good' simply because there were a few pages that gave you a kind of excitement that made you want to find more. If you were then disappointed, the words that caused the excitement did not lose their appeal but could become even more strongly those that made the book special. In *King Solomon's Mines* they were about the two mountains that were 'Sheba's Breasts'. They became the most strangely powerful words of any book I knew.

At the nearest part of the Green to Rod Alley, there was a short path between the road by the Post Office and the one that came down from Fen Street. This made a small triangle of grass that could be used as a boxing ring. Sometimes there would be a boy among the newcomers at the Area School to put on my spare pair of gloves and be an opponent. It didn't happen many times but I liked to think of it as part of what I did at that time. But really I was only dreaming of the lives of the great boxers whose names were coming out of 'the wireless' my parents had recently bought. As well as boxing in England, there was the wonderful set of fights in America, with Joe Louis at the centre, against Max Baer, Max Schmeling, before we had the wireless, then Jim Braddock, Tommy Farr, and Max Schmeling again. Schmeling had beaten Joe Louis in a full length contest in 1935, and

Adolf Hitler had said how a white German had beaten a black man, and this would always be so. The second contest ended with a first round knockout by Joe Louis.

Miss Batley was pretty, but she wore spectacles, and that made us always be less careful to please or obey her than we would have been if she had left her spectacles at home. But, luckily, she had a lovely bosom we could not keep our eyes from following as she stood, or turned, or walked. Her clothes also were good to see, pale blue, pale green, turquoise, well-made, and fitting so her bosom could be loved. But she wore those spectacles. We didn't give her the respect or feeling she should have had. Too easily, we didn't answer quickly enough, or try, or do what she expected. She seemed to have too little confidence. We didn't help her to get it, and didn't know that we should have helped in this. So she would start nagging us to pay attention, or stop this, stop that.

I asked her to put her name in my autograph book. She asked if she could take the book and write more than just her name. She wrote: 'This be the verse you grave for me,/Home is the sailor, home from the sea,/And the hunter home from the hill.'

I thought those words were strange and beautiful. They must have come from some poem Miss Batley loved. She didn't write the poet's name. I didn't ask her, but I wished I knew it.

Twiddy came into the classroom with some complaint about a boy named Cousins. The new school drew children from villages all around, so we mostly were strangers to each other. The matter did not sound greatly important, or we did not realize why it was important, so there was surprise when Twiddy said he would cane Cousins. Then he went out, and instead of taking the boy with him he said he would come back with his stick.

When he came in again, he pushed Cousins forward on a double desk so he couldn't move, swished the cane to frighten us and Cousins, and gave a strong slash across the thin trousers. Cousins cried, and suddenly Twiddy was making fast, hard slashes, each stroke sinking into somewhere near the previous ones, all so viciously that it was hard to believe.

There was silence in the room except for Cousin's crying, and the click of the door as Twiddy went. None of us knew what Cousins had done wrong.

There was a whipping-post in New Buckenham, just two miles away. Under an upstairs room, which was probably a place for village affairs to be settled, the post was in a position where everyone could see it, as a warning. On either side, was an iron bar with manacles shaped in different sizes, spaced up the post, children, women, men. We looked at it with fear, even though it was no longer used. You would have to think that in such a small village it would be the same few people being whipped over and over.

Mr Witham smiled, as if he was always greeting someone. His voice was soft, and he seemed to like it soft, often lowering it still more, so we listened very well. He was dark-haired, and wore spectacles. He was not special to look at, but he was a very special teacher who made us feel special to him.

CHAPTER 25

One dark evening, Neville brought his torch and we went down to Stacksford to spy around the empty house where Grandad Whitehand, had lived, and where he had brought up his family of three boys and three girls after his wife died when they were all quite young. It was a flint-stone cottage and seemed as likely to have a ghost as any empty house we knew. We had to be careful not to draw attention to ourselves as we ventured into the overgrown garden. We put our torches to windows and tried to penetrate the blackness but there was nothing more to see than the sad jumble of old furniture waiting to be shifted. Across the road, the small farmyard was silent, its buildings shut up. Uncle Dick's ferrets must have been squeaking somewhere else.

The old stone house always seemed a sad place because everyone thought of the young mother who had died there. Whenever I imagined it, there were happy young people in my mind, but always in the garden, the boys Willie, Percy, and 'little Dick', the girls Mabel, Kath, and Maud. Perhaps I never placed Willie in the garden, because he would have been away somewhere, working as a youth for Lionel Robinson, the millionaire who had given him a job at the Hall, then William as an officer in the Coldstream Guards during the Great War, then as a farmer at South Walsham, with herds that won cases of medals. Those young ones in my memory garden were always happy because I always imagined them as having friends there too, young men who were keen on the girls, the girls who liked being liked or loved by them. The sad house stayed shut, and it was only occasionally that my imagining let a shadowy figure be standing in it, always silent.

I sometimes thought back to how the Stacksford farm had been when I first knew it. Grandad Whitehand was alone for a while after all his children had grown up. Uncle Dick came each day to look after his ferrets an do a few useful things for his father. The ferrets lived in a box fixed on the wall of a small barn just through a farm gate on the other side of the road, where the meadows in front of the house sloped to the river. Their box had wire-netting on the door, so pink noses poked through, eager for food. Their teeth were dangerous, but Uncle Dick knew what to do. I had to keep my hands away: that was what I knew and did. They had dark and evil-looking little eyes. Their fur was very pale yellowy-white, but brown or black towards the ends, so there were dark patches, one across the middle of the face, one on top of the head, and a big area from the middle of the back to the tail. They liked Uncle Dick's hands and arms. They twisted and turned, and squeaked their happiness. But I never trusted them, their teeth and claws, and liked the moment when he shut them in, to chew and gnaw and squeak and squeal, over and around each other till they tired of it, but when that was I never saw. And I never saw them doing the work for which my uncle kept them, which was to be put into rabbit burrows to drive out the rabbits in fear, so dogs could chase or men with guns could shoot.

Behind the old flint-stone house there was a garden, and, beyond a hedge, the fields that stretched away as far as we could see. The garden was quite small. A little earthen path led from the small gate at the roadside, then turned along the back of the house to the scullery door. There were high lilac bushes shutting off the privy from the house. The privy was different from any other privy I had seen. There was a scrubbed wood seat that had three 'holes', each with its lid, for bums of father, mother, child. The child's was small, and lower, at the further end. I wondered if the privy was ever used like that, all three together. It must have been, occasionally. I went alone, and shut the door, and hooked it carefully.

Beside the privy's nearer end, the path went up the garden, just a path worn there by all the boots and shoes that walked it through the years, Grandad William, Grandma Kate (the one who died), Willie, Percy, Mabel, Kathleen, Dick and Maud, and all before them. Beside the path, about halfway, on the right hand side, there was a place I knew the little dog named Fido had been put the day he died. The rich red stalks of rhubarb grew nearby, with leaves so big you hardly could believe.

I think Uncle Dick only owned one book. It was *The Greyhound Stud Book*. He needed no others because every moment he had at home was spent with this one on his knees. As he was an outdoor man, and Aunt Dolly was an outdoor person too, they didn't have much home time anyway, except for winter evenings. The greyhound book had hard green covers. Uncle Dick loved it and turned its pages carefully, as if his hand was stroking the head of a dog. All the racing greyhounds in Britain were mentioned in it, showing details of their pedigree and owners. Uncle Dick seemed almost to know it all by heart. The dogs were under their racing names, so his favourite dog, Jean, was Buckenham Lady.

When I was younger, Uncle Dick read little books with Wild West stories. They were very thin, with covers of flimsy paper showing cowboy scenes. They weren't the kind of books you keep for years. They were like some books I read at that time, each with a story of Dick Turpin and Black Bess. Most of them were probably not true, but invented from a few facts about him. He was a hero to me in the books, but as I found out more I wasn't quite so sure he should be. The books were tuppence each. They were imitations of the books of Victorian times called 'Penny Dreadfuls', which were usually about criminals.

Dick Turpin was hanged at York. I don't know what happened to Black Bess. I used to have as horrible, strange fear that I'd be hanged too. It said in the newspapers that quite innocent people were sometimes accused. I used to think, suppose I was accused? How can you prove you're innocent if you don't know a thing about what they're accusing you of? I used to think that often. 'Morning, noon, and night,' was what Mum might have said. I never told anyone about the fear. I don't know why. Keeping something to yourself is like feeling guilty, though. That's the trouble with a stupid fear. I just about forgot it, after a while. 'You'll grow out of it,' she might have said, but I never told her. How many people have these fears, and no one ever knows?

Never heard a sound like that,' Mum said, 'when poor Percy broke his leg.'

She was near the Post Office, Percy on the football pitch at the middle of the Green, a hundred yards away. 'That crack,' she said. 'No one would have believed about that sound if they hadn't heard.'

It was likely no one did, but she told the story many times, and it was always fresh to her, so frightening.

Percy recovered, played again. He was a sportsman. What he did best was cricket. Later, he played tennis rather well. But cricket was his love. Like Uncle Dick with *The Greyhound Stud Book*, Percy knew his *Wisden's* just about by heart. But he owned plenty of other books as well.

Uncle Dick gave me a greyhound. It was one of the most beautiful dogs of its kind, a clean-looking fawn, with legs set for speed, a nice pink belly, and the friendliest of eyes. I was the proudest of owners, which was what Uncle Dick wanted. He was obviously very happy that someone in his family should start to follow his interest in greyhounds, and he had no children. But one difficulty in keeping greyhounds is in managing to feed then enough. Their slimness is very deceiving. The pleasure of having Rip came to a sad end. There were two versions of what happened.

He was found beneath the corrugated iron fence at the end of the foundry yard, near Uncle Harry's bake-house. The door was closed. Rip had tried to leap the fence and had been caught on top of it. The bone at the top of one of his hind legs was poking out of the flesh. The vet decided that the injury was too bad for Rip to be kept alive.

Dad's version of the story was different. He said that Uncle Harry had found Rip searching for food in his yard and had frightened him off by swinging the long spade-like implement used for drawing loaves of bread in their tins from the deep oven. Rip must have appeared just at a moment when the old man had the tool in his hand and he swung it in anger, not really intending to do anything more than frighten the dog off. Dad didn't say his uncle had admitted what he'd done, but I think that he probably did, and was ashamed.

With a swinging tin on string, my mother used to go collecting pence for Lifeboats or St Dunstan's blind, every year. Aunt Violet went with a tin I don't know what for, but something she really cared about. Mum told me that when Uncle Percy left school he had a job as an insurance agent, biking round villages to collect a penny a month from people to provide for their funerals.

Grandad Whitehand died. He had not been living in the old house at Stacksford for quite a while because he was not well. Part of the time, he lived with Uncle Dick and Aunt Dolly. Later, he was taken to Aunt Maud's bungalow at Swardeston, which was where he died.

The old stone house was to be sold. Dad remembered the days when it had been the place where he had visited to see the girl he loved, and so he was sad about it being bought by strangers. He decided to try to paint a picture of it for Mum. He took the lid of a shoe-box, cut off the edges, and started work on the clean white underside, with my little set of watercolours and a tiny, not-very-good brush. I don't know how long it took, because I didn't see him working on it. He must have done some of it when I was in bed. He was working from memory, but may have gone back to the house to remind himself of some of the details. He got them right. The flint-stones looked real, the white window-frames, the red roof-tiles, the front door at the centre, the little gate in the left, with the path leading back along the side, a bit of the garden, and the field behind – all like they really were. So he was proud of it, I knew. He didn't show it to us till he had made a frame. It wasn't like an ordinary frame. He made a panel at each end, the picture-glass between them. It was his way of doing it, and it was good. I think it was mahogany.

When it was done, and ready to hang on the wall near the scullery door, in a place where Mum would see it every day, he painted a copy for Aunt Mabel.

From their black frames Grandad Whitehand and his son, Uncle Willie, looked out at us in the front room on the few Sundays the room was used each winter. Apart from those days, they were alone, except when I went in to the tall, glass-fronted bookcase, or Mum came with her yellow duster. Her dusting always included a shine for the bookcase, of which she was very proud because she had found it in a sale when some posh house was emptied, and she always liked time with her black-framed photographs.

Those photographs made the room a sad place. Grandad William had died when he was old, but he had always been a sad man since the death of his wife. Uncle Willie was in his Coldstream Guards uniform, the photograph taken soon after the Great War. Perhaps it was chosen as the picture the family would most want to remember him by, when he died just before the next war.

When there was a good log fire in the grate, we could forget those lost faces for a while, but at most times it seemed to be their room as much as ours. The two armchairs and the couch were covered in stuff patterned with small black and grey squares that added to the gloom. I never enjoyed Sunday much, and not only because of that front room. Few children appeared, except for Sunday school or church. My cousin, 'Big John' went home to Deopham.

We were bought the ten volumes of Arthur Mee's *Children's Encyclopaedia*. Because it was expensive, in beautiful imitation leather covers, it was put in the front room bookcase, and there were so many warnings about being careful with the books that we didn't use them as much as they deserved. My sisters were too young, anyway.

Some of the true stories were unforgettable. The one that stayed with me most strongly was of Grace Darling. She lived in Victorian times. Her father was a lighthouse keeper in the far North, and as she grew up she was able to help, like her brother, with the rowing boat. She was strong and brave, as she had to be. On the occasion that made her famous, she and her father rescued a group of people who survived a shipwreck, in which the vessel had broken in two, and sunk. But soon after that, Grace fell ill. She had tuberculosis, which in those days was known as 'consumption', and for which there was no cure. The cause, said the story, was that most of her time was spent, not in the healthy fresh air, but in a tiny room where there could be no window could be opened because of the sea. Within four years of becoming a heroine, she was dead.

Under a picture in the encyclopaedia, it said 'Abraham Lincoln and his little son, Tad'. That seemed a funny name. I thought of cow tads on the Green. People sometimes said 'cow pats'. We said 'tads'.

'Little Jack Cornwell' is one of the stories you can't forget. He was only just sixteen, and was a gunner in the Royal Navy. In one of the biggest sea battles of the Great War, his ship was fighting off a heavy attack. In all the sound and smoke, the other sailors on his gun were dead or dying, and he was left standing alone, dazed and wounded, and still trying to do his duty, which was to aim the sights of the gun. He died from his injuries a few days later, so he never knew that he would receive the greatest award for bravery, the Victoria Cross, and that he would be remembered when people read books like this.

'There is a Divinity that shapes our ends, rough hew them though we may.'

Often, I liked hearing words whose meaning I didn't wholly understand. There was a preacher who 'held forth' at Baptist chapel meetings out of doors sometimes, on the Green a little way up from Chattergate (where the chapel was on the opposite side of the road). He was a farm worker who had 'got the sack' and went back, as Mum told the story, to his old boss to tell him something in good words.

'The Mills of God grind very, very slowly, Mister Welles-Cole, but they grind exceeding small. And they'll grind you.'

In hymn practice, Hart once ordered me to say what we should sing next. I said, 'The Church's One Foundation.' He said, 'Jesus Christ. Let's have something a bit less mournful.'

There was one hymn tune that we 'belted out' when we were well away from school. It was 'Onward, Christian Soldiers', but we sang the wrong words'. Really, we shouted them: 'Lloyd George knew my fa-ather, / Father knew Lloyd George. / Lloyd George knew my father, / Father knew Lloyd George. ...' It could go on till we tired of it. If we sang it in Cawston's Meetings, we sang the right words, but could still think of the others.

There was a funny word that was about noise. Dad said, 'Turn that dullah off!' when there was something on the wireless that he didn't like. Sometimes, when there was shouting coming from outside, Mum might say, 'What's all that dullah about?'

Alan Gedge came up to me, grinning.

'There's a good picture on in Attleborough next week.'

'What's that?'

"The Elephant's Arse"—in two parts.'

So we laughed together, and Alan went on to tell someone else.

CHAPTER 26

Mr Twiddy came into our classroom, looking serious.

'I have something special to tell you.' We were all looking at him, wondering. His voice was different. 'Mr W B Yeats, the great Irish poet, has just died. He was a very great man and you should know about him. That is all.'

Twiddy must have been very upset, but it seemed strange that he should go from room to room telling children about the death of someone whose name we had never heard.

Mrs Twiddy took us for singing. We had to sing songs that didn't thrill us, ever, like 'The Ash Grove': 'The ash grove, how graceful/how plainly 'tis speaking/the wind thro' it playing/has language for me'. One day, she picked on me to sing that, alone, to the class. They didn't laugh, because every single one of them was afraid she would pick on them if she heard.

The only thing that made those lessons good was the fact that there was a very quiet and pretty girl who was pretty in her own way and unlike anyone else, and she could sing so beautifully, but quietly, that everyone was still and listening, and surely loving her for being so different from the rest of us. It was the most thrilling voice I have ever heard, and I can't even remember her name. She had a song that was supposed to be from a little street flower-seller, asking the passers-by 'Won't you buy my pretty flowers?' She made it so real that we could believe we were there in the street, only to realize, as the song ended, that we were still with Mrs Twiddy and her piano, wondering who would be called out next.

Mr Witham was not the only teacher we liked. Another was Mr Horn. He was mainly the physical training teacher, but in the afternoons he took us for gardening. We couldn't learn much about gardening at that time because the area to be the garden was just rough land, ready for us to clear. So the only gardening we could learn was how to fork up clumps of grass and weeds and knock out the soil. That didn't take long to learn but it took weeks to do and we spent most afternoons at it. In the end we had a nicely laid out set of plots with grassy pathways between.

There was something else we learned. We were being a bit frantic because a bee was buzzing around our heads. Mr Horn became annoyed. 'Stop it,' he shouted. 'Stay still and it will fly.'

'It's on your head, sir,' we said together, still frantic.

'Stay still, I said. It will go away,' he said calmly.

There was quiet while we waited and the bee walked about on Mr Horn's head. Then it stung him and he couldn't help smacking it away, feeling foolishness as well as pain. Perhaps we liked him even more.

Our best times with him were in the school hall which also had to be the gym. Our first lesson in the gym was the first time most of us saw a vaulting-horse and a vaulting-box, and the first time we had seen a teacher going over both. Mr Horn did it with real skill, as he did anything he ever demonstrated in there. He said we would all be vaulting well if we did as he would teach us. But first he had us playing leapfrog over each other's backs. It was true, though, that we were soon clearing the vaulting-horse. The box was something we could land on rather than clear, but Mr Horn had won the respect of all of us.

Mr Horn and Mr Witham seemed years away from men like Hart. Mr Horn had something else that made us think how lucky we were to have him. Somebody realized, and the word soon spread, that a man on a cigarette card of sports champions was our teacher's brother. He was the speed ice-skating champion of Britain.

'I was a seven-stone weakling.'

In a magazine there was an advertisement with a photograph of a perfect-looking man with big muscles all over, holding his hands together in a grip that made arm and chest muscles stand out as much as possible. In the writing there was something about 'the body beautiful' that everyone could have by following the exercise methods of Charles Atlas, the man in the photograph. Write to a certain address, and you could have 'a body like mine'. A booklet came from America, with more pictures of Charles Atlas, and more details of his course of exercises and advice on how 'you too' could get the beginnings of a 'body beautiful' in as little as fifteen days. Keen to try, I thought of little else for a while, wondering how to get enough money to buy the lessons. At last, I knew I could not do that, but I didn't lose interest. Perhaps you could find your own way to perfection. Charles Atlas had found it. I did exercises, and was glad to be in a school where Mr Horn was teaching. He was muscular and very agile when showing us how to vault and do many exercises. But as time passed it became clear that 'the body beautiful' would not come without the Charles Atlas way. 'I was a seven stone weakling,' it said underneath his picture. I comforted myself by being keen on boxing. I was not a seven stone weakling. And I was happy to know that I was not constipated, because constipation was the great evil of modern life.

Mr Nabarro taught me to play the violin. He came each week, with his big nose, his long hair, and his Italian voice. The lessons were at Sunnyside, behind the window on the left, the room quite gloomy, little used. The trees cast shadows in. The lessons were there because we had no piano at home, and Mr Nabarro needed one to 'accompany'. I scraped away at tunes I'd heard, like 'The Londonderry Air', which was better when called 'Danny Boy'. Some that I'd never heard were best because I didn't always realize when I got notes wrong. One called 'Slumber Song', by Schubert, was the best of all. Mr Nabarro was patient. Sometimes he played my violin and showed how good it could be, but that seemed to say something else thing to me. I asked him to write in my autograph book. He wrote some music notes, and underneath them, bold, 'Music hath charms'.

There was a football match against another school. I had begun to be proud of the school I was now in, even trying to design a badge for cap or blazer like those worn in the schools I learned about in the many schoolboy story books I was reading. On the day of the match my good feelings about the new school were strong even though the person who did most of the football training was Twiddy, who obviously fancied himself in that skill. I had never been much of a footballer, and had realized that some of the boys who were not good at school learning were really skilled with a ball.

Much of Twiddy's instruction did nothing to help. He spent his time calling out things like, 'Keep your eye on the ball ... eye on the ball', from a long way off, because he quickly gave up any attempt at trying to move up and down the pitch.

On the day of the match all of that was forgotten. I was keen for my mother to come and stand with me as a spectator. She came quite willingly, but I began to feel embarrassed, as very few spectators had come. At one point, I wondered if she was glad or disappointed about being there. That question led to another which was something like 'How does she look to the other people?' Then I was taken by a feeling that somebody might think that she was odd in some way, perhaps out of place at a football match, because she seemed to be the only mother there.

'Why do you keep looking at me?' she asked. 'You keep looking at me.' That became the only thing I could remember, after a while, about the day of the match.

The lawn in front of Sunnyside had four little garden plots cut into it in the shape of the figures 1808 which made the date the house had two front rooms built on. The plots were planted every year with bright red geraniums, which Aunt Violet took into the safety of the greenhouse when autumn frost began. All summer she mowed carefully round her display. Perhaps it had been there before she was. The same date was set in iron figures on the side of the house that faced to Chattergate.

Patrick O'Malley stole a pig from his father. It was not too bad a thing to do, as he had worked for the old man for a long time for little money. Soon he was on a boat bound for Liverpool. From there he set off southwards, on foot, sometimes stopping for a few days to earn money when chances came, aiming for Birmingham and a job in a factory. How long he worked in factories, I don't know. Perhaps it was not very long, because it is difficult to imagine an Irish farm boy settling for work of factories. It would not have been long before he was on the road again, a tramp, taking himself further down into England, working where he could. Whether he had any aim of getting to the fields and villages of East Anglia, we did not know, but that is where he came, and where he stayed for a while, a man easy to like and quite different from everybody else. He had a job with my father, working around steam engines, corn-threshing drums and straw-pitchers. It must have seemed a good place to be, with people more like those of his home than the factory workers. While he worked with Dad, he lived in one of the living vans. These were built for the engine drivers and other threshing workers taken far from home.

My father liked to tell how, on his fifteenth birthday, he was in charge of a steam engine and the 'threshing-tackle', living in one of the vans. It was in 1915, the second year of the Great War, when the absence of men serving in France had made it necessary for boys to do men's jobs. Twenty-five years later, cars were lessening the need for living vans to be taken where the machinery went, so they tended to be used for workers like Paddy. There were two on the Green, in front of the workshops.

Anyone knowing the appearance of a living van only from the outside, a hut of corrugated iron, on iron wheels without tyres, would have been surprised at what could be seen from the top of the short wooden ladder. Separate upper and lower halves of the door opened on an interior lined with golden pine boards. At one end was a cooking range, with grate and oven, a small version of those in general use in almost all houses. At the other end were two bunk beds. A small table, a couple of wooden chairs, and a box seat for storage, took enough space to prevent the bare floorboards from becoming too noticeable as a place where muck from field and farmyard dropped.

Patrick came to Sunday dinner. It was the first time anyone from the living vans had done so, and it was soon after he arrived in the village. He had ginger hair, perhaps not much for a young man, and it was slicked back smartly. His face was ruddy from life on the roads.

He had bought a second-hand brown suit on Norwich Market. It looked smart and new, and he had scoured himself to redness. He was very good-mannered and polite, and was trying hard to be a good guest. After he had gone, Mum said he seemed to be very awkward with his knife and fork, and she wondered if he was not used to using both together.

One Saturday close to this time, Paddy was in a fight at a pub in Norwich, and his suit was bloodstained. He never again looked as smart as in those early days.

CHAPTER 27

'Guess what! Mr Witham and Miss Batley got married.'

When school began after the Easter holidays, someone started a rumour that soon spread. Miss Batley and Mr Witham had been married while they were away. There was no announcement of the news. Nobody told us that Miss Batley was to be called 'Mrs Witham' now. We hadn't noticed even noticed if the two had been close friends before the holidays. But someone among us said we should no longer call her 'Miss'. 'Please, Miss', 'Yes, Miss', 'No, Miss', had to become 'Please, Ma'am', 'Yes, Ma'am', 'No, Ma'am', from now on.

It didn't work. Miss Batley was embarrassed, angry. 'Stop that, if you please!', 'Don't let me hear you say that again.' Her face was red. But the story was no longer told. Someone had fooled us, and slipped from notice. Who it was, we never knew. Mr Witham and Miss Batley went home separately. Or was that only what we thought? They both lived miles away.

'Nassy' Savoury was really Percy. I suppose he was nicknamed 'Passy' and that got changed to 'Nassy' by some people hearing it wrongly and repeating their mistake, so in the end nobody said 'Passy'.

He was related to me, in a distant way. His mother was the daughter of one of Grandad Loveday's sisters, so she was my Dad's cousin. I suppose that made him my half-cousin. I wouldn't be remembering him if he had not been a Banham boy who had to come to Old Buckenham Area School when it opened. The rule was that all children of eleven and over, from several villages in the area, should come to the new school, and they were given new bicycles to make that possible. The younger children from Old Buckenham came too, but they were in a separate part, the further end of the horseshoe shape.

Another connection I had with Nassy, was that he too was being given violin lessons with Mr Nabarro. Without knowing it, we had both started around the same time. Somebody said that he was learning to play well, which was surprising as he was not very clever at school. When I first heard him play, I was a bit jealous but it was good to know he had found something he could do well. His lessons were being paid for by his grandmother, the person I knew as 'Aunt Alice', who was really Dad's aunt. She also bought Nassy his new violin. My violin was not new. Mine was bought from Mr Nabarro. I didn't ask Nassy if his was too

'That bloody cider,' Nassy said. Our boxing ring was their chicken run. He was on his back, but happy there.

When I went off to Banham, Mum knew where I would be. I had been to the village several times. Uncle Dick had a small place there, his slaughterhouse, with a meadow behind. One day, I'd seen pig killed, then scrubbed clean in a tub of hot water.

The Savoury farm was not far from that place. It was there for growing apple trees for Gaymer's Cider factory in Attleborough. Nassy was glad I'd come. His mother was pleased too. Her eyes smiled through her spectacles. She gave us a drink of cider. It was summertime. We had some more.

Nassy's mother left the rest of the cider so we could help ourselves. When she went in, we just talked a bit, getting to know each other better. Nassy tried on a pair of the boxing gloves I'd brought, amused at himself. I put on the other pair. Nassy said the chicken run could be a boxing ring. It was a few wooden posts with high wire-netting around them. Chickens were up one end, near their nesting house, or in the yard, free to go anywhere. So there was plenty of room for us. Nassy didn't know how to box. I showed him how to move around, on guard, or waiting for a chance to step forward to land a punch or two, then slip away.

He wasn't much good, but we had fun. It was a kind of pretending. I could imagine it as better than it really was. Nassy just liked trying and finding out from someone he knew wouldn't try to hurt him. His mum was in the house and would soon be out if there was trouble. He thought it was great fun, and couldn't help laughing. As he got used to it, he was more confident, and rushed in a bit, swinging his arms, then losing his balance, and losing his breath too. In one of his rushes, I caught him with a punch just as he was about to stumble, and he went down. I knew he wasn't hurt, because he was laughing. He turned on his back and looked up at me, still feeling it was great fun. Then he tried to get up, but couldn't. It wasn't a knockout, because nobody had counted to ten. And there was no referee to decide it was a 'technical knockout' as Nassy couldn't carry on.

'That bloody cider.' he said. It could have been he saw it as a way of getting out of our fight. I was glad we had a way out of it too.

Mrs Twiddy was unchangingly unhandsome.

Her face was big and square, and her hair suited it. Nobody seemed to like her, except one girl who was her favourite, but she liked herself. One day she told the class that she didn't want to live to be very old. It would be better to die before being old enough to suffer in the ways old people did. I wondered if she might change her mind when the time came. It seemed strange for her to tell us her secret.

Mr Witham came to see Dad with an idea that I should try to get into a school in which I could learn more than was possible in the Area School. As a result of this, I passed a test for the grammar school at Diss, and was to start there in September 1939, two years late, at the age of thirteen. Mr Twiddy seemed to think that Mr Witham's belief in me was not good judgement, but he kindly tried to teach me a little algebra at lunchtimes in the next few weeks.

I saw Gabrielle quite often in the summer holidays before starting grammar school. She was usually looking after a small girl named Helen, which gave her a good excuse for 'going for a walk', which meant coming down the road towards Old Buckenham to meet me. Our meetings were eventless ambles along the roadside path, with no outward signs of our attachment, not even in our words, but we were caring strongly, happy to spend time together.

Mr Bush never talked about the Ice Hill, and I never heard anyone ask him about it. Everyone seemed to know of it, but it was not talked of much, except by the few boys who went there. I knew the place well, but as it was on Bush's farm, and not on a part where people were expected to go, we always went there guiltily, trespassing, careful not to draw attention to ourselves as we went down to the end of Church Lane and into the meadow. There, it was sensible to go cautiously so as not to be seen from the back of Bush's farm buildings, which we would have passed if we had made our way through the farmyard from the Green.

Bush was never at the Ice Hill when we went there, but we always saw if he had been working at his task. The hill was supposed to have been a place where food was stored on ice in very ancient times. It was at a place where several fields met. Trees grew around, partly hiding it. Bush was said to believe that the mound was an ancient burial place, and his digging was in search of buried treasure that might have been put in the ground with its owners. He had worked for many hours, but there were no reports that he had found anything at all, and no signs of suddenly greater prosperity in the family. After a while, it was obvious that the treasure did not exist, or that Bush had been unlucky in choosing his place to dig.

Mrs Bush was a maker of good cream cheese, and milk cheese too, for cheapness, so anyone could buy. You had to go up Bush's yard, to buy them at her kitchen door. They were flat and round, one inch thick or slightly more. You carried carefully. They were wrapped in greaseproof paper. Hurry home. They didn't smell like ordinary cheese, tasted better too, except for Red Leicesteshire, my favourite. The cows were milked by Beverley, who' was slightly older than I was. He didn't come out much, except for school. He worked too hard.

Mum went to some evening classes in the Area School. She chose one taught by Mr Witham, on lino-block printing. To give them confidence in something they had never tried before, he encouraged the ladies to print from blocks that had already been cut by someone else. So, after a few weeks, Mum was able to bring home a white tea-time tablecloth with a green-and-orange design round the border. We all said it was nice, but I don't think she ever used it. It was disappointing for her, and us, that she hadn't made the design and cut it herself. I think she thought she should have been bold enough to try. It was likely that she would have gone again the next year, but by then Mr Witham was in the RAF.

Miss Rose was tall and thin, and walked very upright, with arms wide and fingers spread. Children might call behind her, and there were neighbours who troubled her. One man was said to have put something heavy against her privy door, so she had to stay in there until someone moved it. There were other unkindnesses. My mother said that one day when Miss Rose wanted to buy some ribbon in Aunt Gee's shop, she looked in her purse for the money and found she was a ha'penny short. When Aunt Gee heard this, she said the ribbon must be paid for in full before it could be taken away.

'South of the Border' was one of the songs I liked most of all. The story in it was simple, and seemed true. You guess that the man telling it is a cowboy, and you feel yourself in his excitement, and his lying, and then his hope, but also, at the end, his sadness.

> South of the border, down Mexico way,
> That's where I fell in love
> When stars above
> Came out to play,
> And now as I wander,
> My thoughts ever stray
> South of the border, down Mexico way.
>
> She was a picture in old Spanish lace,
> And for a tender while,
> I kissed the smile

Upon her face,
For it was fiesta,
And we were so gay,
South of the border, down Mexico way.

Then she smiled as she whispered 'mañana',
Never dreaming that we were parting,
And I lied as I whispered 'mañana',
For our tomorrow never came.

South of the Border, I rode back one day.
There in a veil of white,
By candlelight,
She knelt to pray.
The mission bells told me
That I mustn't stay,
South of the border, down Mexico way.

A pretty girl with long legs bare and beautiful came down the Council Road on a bicycle with low handlebars. Near the Rod Alley corner, she sat up straight and glided with 'no hands', perhaps showing off a bit to a group of older boys standing near the Jubilee seat on the far side. But she was still going too fast to turn the corner towards Rod Alley Row, and she fell off. We had noticed, from the moment she appeared, that she wore the shortest of shorts. Now, as she fell, she managed not to hurt herself, bounced to her feet. But the boys just laughed and jeered, which seemed not to be the welcome she deserved. She picked up the bike, embarrassed, but carried herself as proudly as possible to Uncle Leslie's gate. Later I found that she was Aunt Ruth's younger sister, Lily, and had cycled from London. In the next few days we got to know her, but I was made too nervous by her attractiveness to talk with her as I would have liked. Soon, Lily was gone, pedalling away to London. There were no lads on the corner to see her go.

CHAPTER 28

'... this country is at war with Germany.' Mr Chamberlain's voice went off. 'God Save The King' was played and Dad said something, Mum said something, and I said, like someone glad, the daft thing that came out, 'The Dutch have took Holland', as if it was thrilling, and Dad shouted, 'Shut up, you little fool. What do you think war is? People get killed in war.' So I shut up and went outside, and didn't come back till dinnertime. I was ashamed, but that was what came out, and what I most remembered of that day, Sunday, September the third, in nineteen-thirty-nine.

Evacuation of children from London at the beginning of the war brought Ronnie Evenden, so my little bed had to take two boys, just at a time when it was becoming too small for one. There were plenty of discomforts, but none as bad as on that first night I had to share with

Ronnie. Whether because of the anxieties of Ronnie's removal from home, or of some problem of my own, one of us pissed the bed, and we woke to a shared dampness for which neither could admit blame.

We were having our Saturday dinner. Suddenly there were screeches of animal pain, in the coal-shed, which was just across a narrow passageway outside the window. Mum rushed out, telling us to stay where we were. After a few moments she came back in great distress because a cat had attacked our guinea-pig, a lovely pure white creature with pink eyes, and left it with its insides showing. She was in tears, saying the only thing to be done was to end the poor thing's misery. Ronnie Evenden said he didn't mind doing the job. He went out to the shed while we sat silent. He came back, pleased with himself.

'I done it,' he said, 'with the chopper. I chopped its head off.'

Mrs Sturman had two evacuees because there was now a spare bedroom, as Hazel had gone to live with her father. One of the boys, Mrs Sturman liked, and always called him by his first name. The other she didn't like from the moment he came, and she never called him anything but 'Isaacs', and always with a sour voice.

In the early days of the war, Major Fildes, who lived in the Manor House, was seeking out men who were suitable for joining the Royal Observer Corps, which was being formed to provide observation day and night of German aircraft that might come over. Dad was invited to join. Mum liked to tell me how Major Fildes had told her he thought Dad was 'the finest-built man in the village'.

The duties of the job were to have several sessions, in three-hour shifts, every week. Dad had a pack of cards from which he learned to identify, in silhouette, any aircraft, both German and British, that might pass over. Messages were passed by telephone, the aircraft tracked, the defences alerted. Dad was enthusiastic about being 'an Observer'. Sometimes he would hand me some cards, tell me to cover the names, and test his knowledge. He soon knew them all. I felt proud of his knowledge, and of holding up Messerschmitts, Dorniers, Focke-Wulfs, Heinkels and Junkers for him to identify.

But, there was one great difficulty for him, which was the fitting-in of times to go 'on duty' at the observer post on New Buckenham Common. Because of his daytime work, the periods of duty had to be at night, except at weekends. One drawback to the weekend shifts, for Mum, was that after the Sunday morning duty, which ended at midday, he liked to go to a pub in New Buckenham and stayed too long, so Sunday dinner had to be late. And sometimes he was late for that.

I didn't decide to stop seeing Gabrielle. She didn't tell me she didn't want me to come to meet her. I didn't even think it was a pity not to be with her. What happened was that when I went to grammar school I had so much 'catching up' to do, because I was starting two years late, and I was covering eighteen miles a day on my bike, so thoughts of Gabrielle were being pushed aside. I was out of touch with her. I even had to go to school on Saturday mornings. After the nine mile ride, there was sometimes a cross-country run in place of lessons.

Uncle Leslie was in his little front garden, wearing a khaki uniform. He looked a bit proud and a bit embarrassed. He was in the L.D.V., which had just been formed for men to defend the places they lived in if the Germans invaded us. The letters stood for 'Local Defence Volunteers', which was thought to be 'a bit of a mouthful', so everyone who talked about them said the 'elldeevee'. But they didn't say it for long, because the name was changed to the 'Home Guard', which everyone thought was better, so men serving in it would be prouder still, though still embarrassed until people got used to it. But, of course, there were some people who were not aware, and went on saying 'elldeevee', which 'just slipped out' because they were 'slow on the uptake'.

On New Buckenham Common, an area of rough grassland for cattle, just beyond the village on the road to Norwich, I met a young man called Maurice Cluer. He came to stay for a few days with an aunt when he was on leave from HMS Ganges, the training ship that often took boys brought up in Dr Barnardo's Homes, usually boys with no parents. On the Ganges, they were trained for the Royal Navy. By the time Maurice joined, it was no longer really a ship, but a large house given the ship's name.

Maurice said he was looking for a special friend for when he was on leave, and I was glad he found me. When he went back to the Ganges, we wrote to each other and became close friends.

It was not long before a letter from Maurice told me of the end of his time on the Ganges and his entry into the Navy. Now I could write to a sailor on a famous ship, HMS Penelope. As it was wartime, he would never be able to tell me where in the world his letters were coming from, as it was always to be kept secret. We tried to work out ways of giving clues, which was exciting but never successful. If anything appeared in a letter that might be a way of telling the secret, it would be cut out by scissors of a censor. There was never a cut-up letter, so Maurice was not taking risks.

'It's enough to drive you shanny,' Mum said sometimes. It was usually when there was something to worry about.

A map came from the *Daily Express,* for me to push in pins, with little flags, to show where battles were, which army held which area. It showed all Northern France, and Holland, Belgium, and a part of Germany. I put it on my bedroom wall, between the door and corner near the window, where the light would make small the print of the place-names readable. I read the news in the *Express,* and listened on the wireless too, so I could know before the next day's paper came. The German pins advanced, the Allies' pins fell back, all silently. After Dunkirk, I left the map up for a while, without the flags.

CHAPTER 29

As I cranked my bike pedals between Shelfanger and Diss, a Spitfire or Hurricane droned its message in the intense blue of a 1940 summer's day.

Early in the war, the Grange, one of the big houses, near the corner of the Green where Mill Road led to Stacksford, was taken over by the Army, and filled with soldiers. Soon after they moved in, Uncle Dick found his favourite greyhound, the only one he kept at home, was sometimes missing for hours if he or Aunt Dolly had left one of their two front doors open. Someone told him she had been seen at the Grange. Dick went to investigate, and found her waiting near the kitchen. He told the soldiers never to feed his dog, and took her home. When this had happened several times, he lost patience. Before long, Jean had departed with some of the soldiers to an unknown place.

Uncle Dick never had one of his dogs in his house again.

Patrick was missing. We watched out for him as the days passed, but he didn't return. Everyone who knew him was wondering why he had gone. We all liked him, all wanted him back.

When the bombing of London lessened, Ronnie Evenden went home to his parents for a 'holiday', and never came back. There was soon a new boy in my bed. I didn't like him. He was younger than me, cross-eyed, and he brought the reputation of having Mrs Gedge from Church Lane tell the evacuee organisers that Tommy Goodgame was too badly behaved for her to put up with any longer. Mum must have accepted him with doubts, but realized a straightening of one of his eyes would be the first step towards changing his behaviour. Within a very short while his mother had agreed to Tommy having an operation. He came back from hospital with a black patch on his glasses and a smiling face. My grumble against him was simply that he was company I didn't want. I wanted my bed for myself. In the front bedroom, with its door next to mine, the bed was empty, except when visitors came. I could have been in there. But Mum had stored many clothes from her younger days in the chest of drawers, and used the dressing-table for recently new things – and she liked to have a pleasant room in case a visitor came unexpectedly.

Uncle George came from Pakefield, on his high-framed bicycle. He would often arrive without warning, stay a few days, then, just as suddenly, depart soon after breakfast, to return the thirty-six miles. One thing we knew about Uncle George was that, a few years earlier, he had been in a motorbike accident and just held on to life in a coma for three weeks. Whenever we went to visit the Bower family by car, which might happen several times each summer before the war, Mum would usually say at a certain point, 'That is where Uncle George had his accident.' It made us 'go quiet' for a while, the little Jowett spinning gently along between high hedges, until something switched our thoughts in a new direction.

So Uncle George and a few other visitors were a good excuse for Mum to preserve her spare bedroom, while I adapted to nights with Tommy Goodgame. One thing everyone agreed on was that the new Tommy with straight eyes was a different boy from the one put out by Mrs Gedge. I tried to live alongside Tommy for the few hours of the night and not have to notice him much in daytime. Sometimes he had things to tell that had to be given attention. A girl had come with him into one of the old privies behind the foundry, ready to be 'felt'. I asked him what he had found. 'It's like jelly,' Tommy said.

'They don't wash,' Mrs Sturman told my mother. 'They just put on their new paint every morning.'

'Isaacs' and the other boy had gone home to London. Now Mrs Sturman had two 'painted ladies' lodging with her, even though her house had only one bedroom large enough for adults, and a tiny room suitable for two children. The ladies had come to be near their children, who were somewhere in the village.

Wilfred Sturman was a man from the Great War. He smiled to me sometimes but hardly ever spoke more than 'John'. This was usually when he came back from long hours and hard work as a gardener at the Hall. He was a short man, with face and hands browned by the outdoor work. It must have seemed odd to him to have two 'painted ladies' in the house. Mrs Sturman was the most unpainted lady to be found anywhere. She always wore a flower-patterned pinafore, ready for her housework, but she always found time for gossip over the garden fence, front or back. The front fence was of neat railings, the back one, of wire netting and a row of gooseberry bushes. For a while, we had a little black and white terrier who found out how to bite gooseberries off a bush. He liked eating them too..

'Hitler—has only got one ball,' ... We went about singing it, to a famous marching-tune called 'Colonel Bogey', which was played by every brass or silver band in England. We knew the tune from often hearing it from New Buckenham Silver Band. As soon as we first heard the Hitler words, they became the only ones to sing, even though there had been other rude ones before. It started as soon as the war began. We didn't know at first that it was not only boys like us who knew it.

'Hitler – has only got one ball!/ Himmler – has something sim'lar, / Goebbels ('Go Balls') has no balls at all!' It was a tune that New Buckenham Silver Band always played very loudly. They loved playing the same things over and over.

There were lost people, many now. One woman was so special that her being lost stood out. Amy Johnson was as special as Amelia Earhart was. She made her flights, broke many records too: Britain to Australia in Gypsy Moth, Britain to Moscow, then on to Japan, London to Capetown, and many more. What we thought of most was how she died. In the war, she ferried planes from factories to airfields of the RAF. It was in all weathers, and the last flight was in the worst kind, In January 1941, from Prestwick in Scotland to Brize Norton, near Oxford. Because of the weather, she landed at Blackpool, carried on next day. Ninety minutes should have brought her to Brize Norton, but over four hours later she came down by parachute in the Thames Estuary. Attempts at rescue failed. She was never found.

'Begin the Beguine' was Neville's favourite tune. He sang (sort of) just scraps of words, and had it on a gramophone record he could sing with, or play his drums. He had real drums, and fancied himself on them, but never took me home to hear him play. I heard him from outside, from 'down the holes', the place of willow trees and brambles, which edged the little road from Chattergate, past Sunnyside. to Wiggy Westfield's corner, which the Petley house was near. When we were young, we both had places to take each other, better than being at home. I had the foundry yard, the orchard, and the workshops. Neville had the 'Old Petley's' White Horse backyard, its outbuildings, and a little meadow behind. Now we were older, we roamed anywhere. He seemed to like 'Begin the Beguine' because it was American. He had other American dance records too He had his drums so he could feel what it was like to play something like Americans played. It was a different America from the one I knew.

So Neville sang his scraps of words. I knew he didn't know much about what the Beguine was, all tropical nights and palm trees under starry skies, and someone not wanting 'them' to begin the Beguine, which I guessed might be a special kind of music, then that someone in the song changing his mind and wanting the music to bring back memories he had not wanted before. It seemed more complicated than the songs I had always loved, but I was a bit jealous of Neville being able to play drums while I couldn't even whistle or play a mouth-organ and had even given up learning the violin when biking to school at Diss and hours of homework had left no time for Mr Nabarro.

Patrick O'Malley came back one winter night. I had spent an evening alone, Mum out at a whist drive, my sisters upstairs, Dad in a pub, still on his way home from work. I heard the front door open and close, and assumed the footsteps in the hall were my mother's. I quickly crouched under the table to give her a moment of puzzlement at finding nobody in the room. Then the inner door opened and I saw a man's boots and trouser legs. My surprise springing-out fell flat and I felt silly, but Paddy was not bothered by that. Rather, he was relieved at not having to make explanations to my parents about why he disappeared, months earlier, and why he was now standing in our doorway again. I was delighted to have him there. The copy of *The Family Doctor* in which I had been reading about all my imaginary symptoms, could be shamefacedly closed and hidden, and appendicitis put off for some future panic hours.

'He would worry the worms out of a nag's arse,' Mum said. I forgot who it was she was talking about but knew it must be a saying she had heard long ago. She often said things about people worrying, because it was what people often did. 'Worry-gutting' was what she mostly called it when anyone bothered her with worries not serious enough to matter. And, 'It's enough to worry anyone's guts out,' was another favourite, when it *was* serious.

I went to Norwich Hippodrome with Neville to see Al Bowlly. When we were younger, we had known many of the songs he sang, but, of course, many of them were sung by other singers too. He was very much liked by the audience in the Hippodrome, and as most of them were older than us, they had known more about him than we could know.

There was also a kind of sadness in the theatre, because everyone knew that Al Bowlly was a man who had been very famous and popular in America as well as Britain, but now, as they listened, as he sang 'Goodnight Sweetheart', 'Love is the Sweetest Thing', 'Blue

Moon', 'I've Got You Under My Skin', 'My Melancholy Baby',, 'The Isle of Capri', and 'It's a Lovely Day Tomorrow', people were thinking how sad it must be for him to know that his great days were gone, and he had to remember them as he sang, and that the applause we gave was only a reminder of how many more hands had clapped in other times.

One night, thunder was so very near, but it was outside, up there, even if it was right overhead.

Mum came along the landing, opened my door, switched on the light.

'Thunder and lightning, aren't you scared ?' she said. I said I wasn't.

'I am,' she should have said. 'The girls are sound asleep,' she said. She switched the light off, said, 'It's safer off,'

She stayed a while. Dad was on duty with the Observer Corps. She went nearer to the window, nearer, looking out, saying things like, 'Oh, listen to that. Here comes the rain...It's going over, isn't it? Well, that was something, wasn't it?'

She put the light on, smiled, clicked off, and closed the door. Her feet along the landing, rain, the rain, the lightning further off, thunder only, grumbling.

CHAPTER 30

I was at a gymkhana in Watton with Neville. There was some time when we were not needed in the ring, so we were free to look around at the various sideshows. In one quiet place, away from where people were passing, a young woman sat near a hedge, giving her breast to a baby. I had not intended to stare at her. She was with another girl, and did not mind that I could see. Perhaps she was pleased, because she must have realized that this boy was seeing one of the best things he ever saw.

Patrick O'Malley was a man of surprises. One day he said he would show me how to sew a sole on a boot. What he meant was that he would teach me to do it. Perhaps he assumed that one day I would be leaving home rather as he did, with no way of travelling but on my feet. His boots needed soling, so he had bought some leather for the job. He took out from among his small pile of possessions a strong needle and thread. He made a few holes with a bradawl, some in the sole, others in the boot, and started to sew. In a short while, the stitches were in a neat pattern, which he showed me with obvious pride.

'Now you have a go.'

As much as lack of any skill, for me, a difficulty was in the strength needed for pushing in the needle. But Paddy was a patient teacher who truly wanted me to be able to fix a sole. I suppose I made a few passable stitches, but the boots of a man of the roads must have no weak places, so Paddy soon took over again, and I was able to sit wondering at his skill, knowing that there are lowly, humble things to admire. There was another thing that Paddy could do that was not at all lowly or humble.

He could say the whole of a famous book-length poem by heart. 'Sweet Auburn, loveliest village of the plain' … I had my school book of Oliver Goldsmith's *The Deserted Village*. It tells the story of a village moved by a landowner to another part of his estate, regardless of the wishes and attachments of the people who lived there. It is a thing that happened in several places, probably in many more than those that came to light. Paddy was delighted to see the book, and told me proudly that he could recite it all, remembering from the learning of his schooldays. Perhaps there had not been much forcing, because he obviously took great pleasure and pride in it, even if knowing it all by heart might have been an exaggeration. The only other person I knew who could remember long poems was my mother. When I was eight or nine, she recited several of them so many times that I learned long passages of them.

It was a summer evening,
Old Kaspar's work was done,
And he before his cottage door
Was sitting in the sun,
And by him sported on the green
His little grandchild, Wilhelmine.

She saw her brother Peterkin
Roll something large and round
Which he beside the rivulet
In playing there had found;
He came to ask what he had found,
That was so large, and smooth, and round.

Qld Kaspar took it from the boy,
Who stood expectant by,
And then the old man shook his head
And with a natural sigh,
' 'Tis some poor fellow's skull,' said he,
'Who fell in the great victory.'

I knew that one by heart: all eleven verses.

There were quite a lot of funny poems that start off with the first line of a proper poem my mother had told me. This one did:, but I didn't hear it from my mother 'The boy stood on the burning deck,/The weather it was rippin', /Miss le Neve lay on her back,/ And on her crack was Crippen.'

The older lads who used the Jubilee seat as their gathering-place had mostly left, their damage done, and moved off to other ways of spending their spare time. Some had joined the army or RAF or navy, or gone for war work in other parts of the country. Some, in the Royal Norfolk Regiment, had been captured by the Japanese, after the fall of Singapore, and were prisoners.

The damage to the seat had been small at first, a single broken slat, where some careless lad had slammed his heel-cap hard, in showing-off or something similar, half-accidental. Other slats were broken deliberately, once the damage had begun. If there were any lads who disapproved, they would not have spoken-up. It was too likely to be thought 'wet' or 'goody-goody'. People started saying the seat 'looked a disgrace'. Where the pieces had broken away, the weather did its further damage. You thought that Japanese oak couldn't be as strong as English, anyway. Nobody sat there.

Mum was amused when she told me of something she had asked Patrick.

'Have you thought of going in the army, Paddy?

'What, you want me to get killt?'

Patrick's greatest surprise was when he disappeared again. This time, he didn't just go without a goodbye. He went on my father's bike. Perhaps the biggest surprise about his going was not that he rewarded all the help and kindness by stealing the bike, but that he was missed with sadness because we knew that, this time, he could not come back. We wondered if he returned to Ireland, and, possibly, paid his father for the pig.

'Sink the Bismarck,' said Winston Churchill. The story was on the radio and in the newspapers of how the greatest warship in the German navy was chased from near Denmark to the Atlantic by many British ships. The Bismarck had sunk a long-famous ship, HMS Hood, and Churchill had given an order in great bitterness. The Bismarck was reaching open sea, but suddenly turned south, heading for the greater safety of the harbour of Brest. Time was getting short for the British ships, and the greatest match for Bismarck, HMS George V, was short of fuel. I was thrilled to know that my friend Maurice Cluer was a leading seaman on George V, and tried to imagine how the story seemed from wherever he might be on board. Guns, torpedoes, bombs from Swordfish planes, all played a part, and in the end the Bismarck sank. I learned without Maurice ever needing to say, that there was always so much feeling for the sailors who were drowned when any ship 'went under', that it was decent not to talk about it much.

A girl from a nearby farm came sometimes, on horseback, to call on Mr Oliver. Like him, she took horses to gymkhanas, and took home rosettes on bridles. Neville and I were too much aware of her classiness to dare to show our responses to her in anything more than what we said to each other about her. Only a glance, or even more, sometimes, a gentle smile, could prompt longings we knew we should keep hidden. She was not for us, we knew well, and if she had shown a wish to know us better we would have been too scared to act. The ideal situation to occur would be for her to look to us for a boy's strength or expertise at something practical, something like a helping hand with a horse, but the fact was that there never was the slightest need of help or advice. We were only village boys receiving Mr Oliver's kindness, nothing like her equals in any way, and we never wanted to be her equals, only to feel the excitement of being noticed by her, and daring to let the slightest hope that we might be attractive to her hold our thoughts for as long as it could.

My cousin Russell was evacuated from the coast about a year after the war began. He came to Diss to live with our Aunt Allie, landlady of The Star, so now we were at the same school. Sometimes on Friday he might bike home with me for the weekend. As we left Diss, we passed a small farmhouse where his sister Olive had come to live. Going through Shelfanger, he once told me that he wanted to become a novelist. I knew he had been very keen on the Tarzan books by Edgar Rice Burroughs, and for an instant that Norfolk road was surrounded by jungle, in which Tarzan was swinging on a long vine from tree to tree towards a beautiful girl.

One Saturday, Russell and I went to work with Dad and did a dusty 'chaff job' round the threshing machine, on Mawby's farm. At the end, we were each paid one shilling and sixpence. Dad was angry. He told the farmer we'd been underpaid, came back with two half-crowns. Dad 'never had much time' for mean people. His usual saying about them was, '.Too mean to tell a blind boy the time'. I never heard anyone else say that, so I thought he had made it up.

Biking through the dark for hours, with shaded headlights to throw their tiny disk of yellow to the road, we made our way from Old Buckenham to Pakefield in the wintertime of 1941, shoulder to shoulder mostly, Russell and me, with no more sense between us than these facts show. Though I knew the road somewhat, from pre-war outings in my dad's small Jowett, and Russell had the lure of home, this thirty-six mile journey, as it should have been, in the night by war time 'blackout', with all signposts down for confusion of 'the enemy', was not the trip we thought it would be when the notion of it came. We lost our way somewhere near Bungay. Not long after that, my left pedal slipped to an angle and fell away. Found, it could not be fixed back. I cranked like Cookie on my one good leg, the other hanging. Swapping bikes sometimes, with nothing in the sky to guide, we came to somewhere near the coast, but too far south, so turned to the left and came to Pakefield in the early hours, into Grand Avenue, grand in width but, until quite recently, a sandy track, with bungalows and houses on either side. All were now curtained and blinded, and all the sleepers' lights were out. Russell tapped a windowpane.

CHAPTER 31

Someone new was in the lives of Uncle Dick and Aunt Dolly. He was an evacuee from London. His name was Teddy Vidler. He settled in with them so happily that everyone noticed. Teddy was liked by everybody, and the little Whitehand house had children hanging around outside, looking for their friend. They began to use Teddy's way of talking to 'Uncle Dick'. Soon, every child seemed to know my uncle as 'Uncle Dick', and nobody thought that odd.

'Dick was up the garden,' said Aunt Dolly, 'and the door blew off.' She was talking with Mum about a great storm the day before.

I said, 'Was it the door?', and Aunt Dolly laughed the way we always thought of as her way of laughing. Her face was red and her whole body shaking.

'Oh, John,' she said.

Mr Crane rode the tallest bicycle in the village. He was the tallest man in the village, by far. His body and his legs and arms were too long. They looked too long whether he was riding his bike or pushing it. Usually, by the time he was nearing home, where I saw him, he was pushing it. Besides being of great length, he was also thin, his old brown suit close-fitting. His head was small. He never looked sideways much, as if he might see in our faces our thoughts of himself. When people spoke of him, it was usually of Rat Crane, but we didn't know if he knew of this cruel name.

He lived with his sister, in one of the better houses after the corner of the Green on the Attleborough road. It was called The Laurels. Most of our homes didn't have names, or numbers. Names were usually given only to the posher places, the Manor, by the corner leading to New Buckenham, the Grange, by the corner leading to Stacksford. Others with names were Sunnyside, Sunnyside Farm, and The Laurels. Most of the farms had names too.

Miss Crane, who was posh, must have been embarrassed that her brother was so oddly-shaped and rode or pushed his suitable tallest bicycle, (She would have spoken it properly: 'bicycle' not 'bike'.) She had a friend, Nurse Cooley. People said how much they liked each other. The nurse was a big and bosomy lady in a dark blue uniform and hat, pink-faced and busy-looking. Miss Crane was very different, older, in dowdy browns and greys, posh persons' clothes. Both ladies lived beside a different road out of the village. Nurse Cooley's bungalow was beside the New Buckenham road, and new. She had a little car, to do her work as 'District Nurse'. When I was 'six and a bit', I came home from school at dinner-time one day and found 'Old Lady Etteridge', Afred Etteridge's grandmother, was 'doing things to help', like getting dinner ready, and the nurse was coming down the stairs to tell me something. My mum had a new baby, my sister Barbara. I didn't remember any more of that.

When I was nine, and home from hospital, with adenoids and tonsils out, and feverish, Nurse Cooley came again, to give me an enema. I didn't know what an enema was, but soon found out. Until then, I'd only had 'a spoonful of Syrup of Figs, or a fizzy drink of powder in a glass of water, which was Andrews' Liver Salts, and, only once or twice, and horrible, some Epsom Salts. These were things for Friday night, and things you didn't tell your friends. Even more, you wouldn't tell about an enema. They would have said, 'What's that?'

Mr Crane was not alone in having a cruel nickname. There were many nicknames, kind or unkind, some quite cruel. A list of some remembered easily will show: Manny Bush, Naff Etteridge, Sudden Rudd, Stoot Loveday, Long Lincoln, Hinny Bray, Podger Fisk Tip Self, Fiddler Wright. Pippin Elvin, Ritty Ward, Brother Fox, Wiggy Westfield, Cuckoo Loveday, Lugs ...

A boy from New Buckenham was called 'Lugs' because he had very big ears. We even called him that as the usual way of speaking to him, and without meaning it unkindly. We could even say it in a way that made him feel liked by everybody, as he was. His real name was Cecil or it could have been Cyril. We didn't use it enough to remember.

The air-raid siren sounded and there was soon the drone of German bombers passing over. We thought that we could recognize 'the enemy' by that distinctive sound. A small group of people outside in Rod Alley Row was held by the thudding bombs or anti-aircraft guns from the direction of Norwich. For this hour there was the strange feeling of seeing events we needed company to share.

Bert Jackson, a burly foreman from the workers who were building the new airfield at the top of Abbey Road, came round the corner from the living van he was hiring, and stood among us. I noticed he was shivering with fear. I couldn't stop watching him. He was a man of strong looks, very much like the Western film actor Andy Devine, and he was shivering with fear.

'Germany calling ... Germany calling,' were the opening words of a regular daily wireless programme that people found they could hear coming from Germany, specially for British listeners. The voice was of William Joyce, who became known as 'Lord Haw-Haw'. We soon got to know that our Government hated the broadcasts because they were full of lies about German victories and achievements, and British defeats and failures, but it was really obvious that many of Lord Haw-Haw's stories were lies. When we listened, it was very easy to feel that this pompous voice was something to laugh at, and his stories were unlikely to be true. But among many people who 'tuned-in', there were many likely to have reason to worry because they had friends or relatives in danger, and some who were in danger themselves.

All day, the sun on the foundry yard, on corrugated iron roofs of shelters for the seasoning wood, on a threshing drum, the early Ford, on elder, nettles, the orchard, on *Lavengro.* The book was thick and old, one Grandma found somewhere. Her sons or daughters left it long ago. Its covers were plain red. No pictures showed the characters. George Borrow tells his story of strange people met as he tramped the roads and lanes of England in the early nineteenth century. I was fifteen, sprawled in the grass (where, years before, I wore the redskin girl's green dress). Now, I followed far-off dusty roads to Mumpers' Dingle, where the strange tall girl with the striking name sat in her tent, the man who tells it all, Lavengro, talking with her, and I listened, spellbound, because they were spellbound too, each with the other's talk and charm, and Isopel Berners was a name to whisper in my head, and feel her spell.

The book was written by George Borrow, who had been born at East Dereham. He was Lavengro. The first sentence of the book made me want to read on. 'On an evening of July, in the year 18--, at East D---, a beautiful little town in a certain district of East Anglia, I first saw the light.'

A policeman was in our front yard with my mother when I came home. He was there to ask me questions about the man who lived in one of the living vans. 'Mr Jackson,' he said, 'I want to ask you something about him.' I can't remember how he said it, but it was something about the way he might be 'touching' boys. He asked if this man had touched me 'like that'. I said he hadn't. Mum looked pleased, as if an answer she had already given had been the right one. I knew what the officer meant, but I thought it was something I didn't want to do, to put someone in danger of disgrace because of a moment of stupidity. It seemed that some boy had told his mother something, but I gave the impression of not knowing what was being talked about.

A woman they called 'Crazy Kate', large, with ginger hair and a rhubarb leaf laid over it, stood at her gate in Winfarthing, as I was nearing, biking home. She opened the gate, came out, and walked along the road edge, dressed in a vest and pale blue skirt. Her great breasts bulged, perhaps quite beautiful. Why on earth I told my mum the story is lost from memory. When she repeated it, the skirt was gone. I think I must have told it so, but she liked a story to be remembered.

In the little room', alone, I was sitting at a small, round-topped table, with the little dark-haired monkey, stuffed for a century or more, and holding up his sloping branch that had become a support for an electric table-lamp bulb. Mum had bought him at a jumble-sale. I disliked him because he was dead. He had a slight smell about him, the effect of the light bulb's heat on his dusty hair. Now, he was my only company as I did homework in the quiet of the room that was once a place of fairies appearing from scribbles, and adventures opening up in pages of comics and 'annuals'. He had glass eyes and could not share my boredom, or my belly discomfort as I delayed going 'up the yard' with a torch to the stinking 'lav'.

Almost everything that I found in the grammar school was as dead as this monkey. I started there two years late, and struggled to catch up. Two teachers stood out, the young French mistress for delighting in her own comeliness, and being able to move me quickly upwards in the end of term lists, and Mr McMullen, who taught such poems as Oliver Goldsmith's 'The Deserted Village' and 'When You Are Old' by W B Yeats. One poem linked McMullen to Paddy O'Malley. The other made me realize what even Twiddy had been touched by. Mr McMullen read us 'When You are Old'. I remembered Mr Twiddy coming into our classroom at the Area School two years earlier, to tell us that WB Yeats had died.

> When you are old and grey and full of sleep,
> And nodding by the fire, take down this book,
> And slowly read, and dream of the soft look
> Your eyes had once, and of their shadows deep.
>
> How many loved your moments of glad grace,
> And loved your beauty, with a love false or true,
> But one man loved the pilgrim soul in you,
> And loved the sorrows of your changing
>   face;

And, bending down beside the glowing bars,
Murmur, a little sadly, how love fled
And paced upon the mountains overhead
And hid his face amid a crowd of stars.

Everyone listened intently as Mr McMullen read. I loved the poem straight away. Although we were so far off from being old, it was something fascinating, although perhaps with a bit of fear mixed in. It was also a love story, which was something we could now imagine having for ourselves.

The ending was kind of romantic, with the idea of the poet being someone special. I might have thought it a bit fanciful, but I can't be sure. Mr McMullen put most of his feeling into attacking, quite angrily, a misprint in the school text-book. It was 'ridiculous!' Instead of saying the poet 'hid his face amid a crowd of stars', the book said *crown* of stars.

'How can you hide a face amid a *crown*?' he laughed. 'Idiot!' He said he thought it was a daft mistake by an editor, not a misprint at all. Poetry was special, he meant. You didn't have to try to make it special by writing 'crown' rather than 'crowd'.

Mr McMullen came over to my desk as I was about to follow the others out of our last lesson of the term. He had a book with a dark cover in his hand.

'Something you might like to read. There are two plays in here. O'Casey. Sean O'Casey.'

As he said the name, his voice sounded somehow more Irish than usual. And I liked that.

The summer holidays stretched ahead. I felt pleased he had singled me out. It was meant to show he thought of me as already likely to enjoy the kind of writing he bought for himself. But all these thoughts were in the one moment of not knowing what to say, except 'Thank you, sir', as he put the book on my desk.

I read the plays from the moment I got home. They were 'Shadow of a Gunman' and 'Juno and the Paycock'. They made me feel like an adult reader, because they had been lent to me by a man who expected me to understand them, and take something from them that would lead me on to other books.

And there were other books – all Irish – to follow. I wondered if Mr McMullen sometimes felt lonely, cut off from his own people. There couldn't have been many of them in Diss.

But education came from people far from school.

There was a man in New Buckenham we called 'Brother Fox'. I don't think we ever said it to him but only in talking about him. He would have been quite happy if we said it in his hearing, smiling and giving a small grunt of approval.. We liked his company and he liked ours. He was greatly tolerant of our behaviour as it edged towards talk or behaviour that adults didn't usually approve, like 'smut' or smoking. His bicycle shop was a place to gather in. There was no need to spend money, and we could stay as long as we liked, as cigarette stubs gathered on the floorboards. He even gave us cigarettes if we had none. For anyone from our own village, Brother Fox's was probably the person we liked most in this one.

Russell has come for a few days at Old Buckenham. We are cranking home with Cookie from 'the pictures' in Attleborough. It's getting dark, the time for 'lighting up', but we're taken by surprise, caught out, without lights on our bikes. On Gaymer's Corner there's a group of 'special constables'. They are men who have other jobs but work as policemen in their spare time, so they don't make us nervous like real police.

'Where are your lights?'

To shout, 'I'm going home to get them', seems so right to answer, cheeky too, enough to rile him, rile them all. Will they give chase?

Cookie takes his chances, pedals off as if he has two perfect legs. I'm following, with Russell beside me. The men stay in the darkness, let us go. No chase. It seems a little victory, the law a little broken, something accomplished.

There was something in the 'EDP' about Bert Jackson. He had been sentenced to six months in prison. I thought of Bert in a cell in Norwich, and felt sorry for him there, among the criminals. He didn't seem to be a criminal, just a man who 'went astray', as Cawston's Meetings always said we do. I thought of something he had said: 'I can give you something better than any woman can.' It seemed an oddish thing to say. I didn't know that much about what a woman might do, anyway. I hadn't thought too much about it then, supposed I would in time. It was out there in the future, still a good way off. Bert might find his way to something too. He seemed only a foolish man, and kind of frightened in some way. I thought of when we stood and watched the air-raid going on, and he was shivering with fear.

Uncle Dick paid me half-a-crown every week for exercising some of his greyhounds. They were kept at his premises in Banham, in a yard behind his slaughter-house. He was busy wartime work as the only butcher for miles around to be licensed to slaughter animals for food, so he had little time for attending to his dogs.

Biking home from Diss, I took the road to Banham from Winfarthing, instead of the usual one. It gave me a longer bike journey, by about two miles. From Banham, I walked four dogs, on leads, first, a mile towards Old Buckenham, then turned away towards Kenninghall for another mile, and another back into Banham, only to be exhausted by a final three miles, biking home. The half-crown was good to have on Friday night, but it was hard-earned.

Mum went to evening classes again. This time, it was on making lamp-shades. She made two. There were copper wire frames, and in each square aperture a sheet of tough parchment was fixed. The idea was that the next stage was for her to paint designs in the panels, but Dad became interested, and offered to paint birds on them. He searched in the Children's Encyclopaedia to get the details right, then worked with the paint brush in such a concentrated way that he suddenly had a 'blackout'. We were very worried for a few moments, but he came back to consciousness and insisted he was all right. We knew he was working too hard, by day and night, because of his duties in the Royal Observer Corps, which always came after a hard day's work in the business. Sometimes, especially on Sunday afternoons, he might be irritable, saying things like ; 'I'll paddle my own canoe', which seemed a nice way of saying, 'I shall please myself'.

Maurice Cluer, on leave from his ship, was with me in our front yard. He indicated the little road by the iron railings.

'If my mother walked along here now, I wouldn't want to know her.' I didn't know why he said it at that moment, and didn't know what to say. We carried on talking as if he had not said it, and he never spoke of his mother again.

CHAPTER 32

Greta sat with me in the long dry grasses. We were in the meadow at Sunnyside, in the middle of which the tennis court had been created many years earlier. I expected her to be uneasy and wanting to play tennis rather than to sit and talk. I knew that if we played she would win easily, so I was in no hurry. Then she said something about the rudeness of boys at Thetford.

'He says things like "Get in there, knob: it's your birthday".'

On the voice of this girl, the words seemed as surprising as if flesh itself has been uncovered. But, at the same time, she was entirely protected in innocence because she had only quoted something of which she seemed to disapprove, though with a relish of the embarrassment she was causing me. We talked on in the afternoon sunshine, and did not play tennis. Nor did we venture any further with the dangers of innocent words, but there was a pleasure and a wariness that played between us until it was time to go.

I left school without gathering the courage to ask, Mr Fairs, the headmaster, to return the book on the slave trade I had lent him about a year earlier. Perhaps he had not really wanted to borrow it and didn't like to say no to the offer, but, if so, he could have returned it after a short time. Perhaps he had realized it was quite valuable, perhaps really valuable. It was a very early book, written when slave trading was truly a problem. It had come to our house when my mother was collecting old books that could be sold for 'the war effort'. We had piles of them in our coal-shed, most of them dumped simply because they were ancient, almost falling apart, not worth anything, meant for paper salvage. Dad sorted through and saved a couple of early printings of Shakespeare plays. But he liked the slave trade book especially, and was forever reminding me to bring it home. But perhaps it had no worth.

Something I remembered from a Shakespeare volume was the character in *The Tempest* who, on getting out of a pond he had fallen in, exclaims, 'I do smell all horfe piff'. In the school-book text for School Certificate, he said, 'I do smell all foul water'.

Mr Fairs said 'Traffle-gar'. He never told us why. Was it the way the Spaniards said it? We never asked him, never pronounced it as he did. And nobody else did (those we knew). Perhaps everyone in England always said it wrongly, except a few that Mr Fairs had taught before he came to us, some Harrow boys.

Dad liked using long words. Although he had been forced to leave Norwich School for Boys at the age of fourteen, after only one year there, because of the outbreak of the Great War, he had not given up wanting to be educated. He was encouraged in this by his elder sister, Hilda. She was good at finding books that would interest him in the thoughts and ideas of great philosophers' He became proud of them showing in a bookcase he and Mum brought home from a house sale they went to at Swardeston. It was of rich dark red wood, and had glass panels in the doors, and a cupboard below. He sometimes said how he had read the *Ethics* of Spinoza, and John Stuart Mill's *On Liberty*, and I found them in the bookcase.

Some of the big words Dad used were 'concatenation' ('concatenation of events') and 'quandary'. When he was uncertain whether I should leave school, he wrote to Mr Fairs, saying that he was 'in a quandary' about it, but he made a mistake and wrote 'quandarary'. Mum was embarrassed. She showed me the letter, which he had left on the table, and asked me what I thought of it, because it was written on a Sunday afternoon when he had come home late from the pub in New Buckenham, where he went, as usual, after his three hours of duty with the Observer Corps.

I was sixteen. I persuaded myself that I wanted to be a civil engineer, which meant that I became a trainee at the new water-works on the high ground at the top of Abbey Road for twenty-five shillings a week.

Much of the time was spent in digging, shovelling, pick-axing, helping to make trenches across roads and up gardens in order to connect houses to the water supply. I often worked with Walter, a short, rosy cheeked, bespectacled man of about twenty-five. He was good company, teller of smutty jokes which we both thought funnier than they really were.

Walter said I should be careful about what I might try to do with girls, 'because tha's got teeth in it'

Listening to Walter, I was filling in some of the empty spaces in my education. One day we stopped our work to stand in respect as a funeral procession passed.

'It won't always be some other bugger in there,' Walter said.

When Olive came to stay with us as a mid-teenager, she seemed even more attractive than ever, and it felt good to be with her. We were sitting on a log on the Rod Alley side of the

Green, not far from the steam engines. She took off her blouse and showed the red bathing costume underneath. I dared her to walk across the Green, dressed like that, knowing how surprised anyone seeing her would be. She laughed, as if it might be fun to startle people who were so easily startled. When she was at the far corner, near the Stacksford road, she turned and started back. I admired her, and was strangely excited by such a small act of daring as she came towards me.

At another time, I took Olive for a walk, to show her a part of the village she didn't know. It was along a wide pathway through the Stud, past the fenced paddocks and the stables, and out at the far end near Mr Horsefall's farm.

When we reached the farm, there was a new straw-stack by the edge of the field opposite the farmhouse. Part of it, at one end, was low, inviting us to sit for a while before starting home. We lay back, closing eyes against the sun. A few men on bikes went by, so it was 'leaving-off' time. We trudged back, happy. When Dad came in the back door, he was amused. A man had told him, 'Your boy John is in a straw-stack with a girl'.

Occasionally, I was sent out from the waterworks on my bike to turn on stopcocks at the roadside in villages for several miles around. The purpose was to prevent stale water from building up in places where the few houses connected to the supply might not take off enough water to keep it at good quality. It was a lonely job, but I liked it. It gave me a sense of importance because I was relied upon to do it well. A heavy iron rod, the 'key', was strapped to my crossbar, a weight that made pedalling harder uphill but would help me to whizz downhill. A slight turn on the stopcock would send gushing water along the roadside, and I would have to wait several minutes at each place.

I bought a brown 'trilby' hat that I thought would add maturity to my appearance, not realizing that I looked fairly silly in my pretence. It was a really nice trilby, with braided silky hatband in a lighter brown. I usually couldn't resist wearing it in the evenings, and nobody told me it looked silly, but nobody said it looked good either.

I began to imagine what I would look like in a few years time. It had no connection to how I looked then, nor to any way I might appear even if I became a senior civil engineer. The chap I wanted to become was dressed in obviously expensive clothes, not a suit but jacket and trousers very well matched, in good material. Most times, there was a pile of books under one arm, and I was hurrying somewhere they would be used, somewhere I never quite got to.

The cause of these fantasies was John Hampden Jackson, who came each week to give a talk for the WEA (Workers' Educational Association, but nobody used that 'mouthful', as my mother might have said) in the Village Hall, a wooden building built for the young men back from the War in 1918, a short way down the Attleborough road. He was a lecturer from Cambridge University, author of history books, who was keen enough to drive each Wednesday a round trip of ninety miles to talk to us, just over a dozen ladies and a man and boy. I was the boy. Jack Kemp the postman came because his union paid his fee. The ladies were serious-minded, thoughtful ones, though some would have kept coming because they liked the lecturer. I was there because I needed something more than digging trenches with Walter, something of other lives. That autumn, the course was on the Soviet Union, because of happenings in the war. The last part of each class was 'question time'. John Hampden Jackson put questions to us to encourage us to ask our questions too. He smiled, called me 'the boy with the School Certificate'. I knew that it was playful, intended to make the ladies smile, but I never resented it. I sensed a kindliness in him, and felt close to it.

Odd, inconsequential memories survive much more than those we paid our small fees for. JHJ went through the whole of one session with his 'flies' undone, probably the only person in the room quite unaware. But, week by week, this man touched us with his knowledge and his eloquence.

I hadn't seen a nude before, and when we went to Norwich on that Saturday I didn't dream I would see a dozen before Dad took me home. We'd come, bringing Uncle Leslie, in the car. They were there for business in the Corn Hall, selling seed they'd threshed, by showing specimens. I would be free to please myself where to go. After we'd had some fish and chips, Dad told Uncle Leslie he could manage on his own if Leslie would like to take me to the Hippodrome. Leslie knew Dad really meant he'd like to do some of the business in a pub. So, not a drinking man, he said it was a good idea. But he didn't know what show was on. We soon found out. As we went through the theatre door the seats were filling. We stood up several times to let men pass. Musicians played. The fire curtain went up. The lights went out. The music changed. After a few moments, a spotlight picked out a figure at the side. There was applause. The spotlight and music brought her on, in a flowing gown, to centre stage. A voice announced, 'Miss Phyllis Dixey'. There was applause. She waited, smiled, enjoyed it, welcomed us. When it was quiet she said something in a rhyme about 'The Girl the Lord Chamberlain Banned'. She and her girls would show us 'tableaux', themselves displayed to show great paintings 'brought to life'.

I didn't know enough about art to recognize the pictures shown, but when the stage went dark and each new tableau was arranged before the lights came on again, there was a certainty of knowing what the light would bring, and how good it was to be there watching, looking in on something rare, in almost disbelief.

It was a first time. You could get used to it, someone might say afterwards. We met Dad somewhere. I can't remember where it was, or what Uncle Leslie said of where we had been. There was darkness in the car, dim wartime headlights moving intermittently towards us in the dark outside, the little spotlight patches, coming, passing by

As I passed the blacksmith's shop, Edgar came out to tell me something.

'John, your grandfather is a great man.'

He said it as if it was something I should know. I didn't know what to say, except a confused 'Yes'. Afterwards, it seemed a special occasion, one very old man wanting to praise another, his neighbour in business for over half a century, as both came towards the end of their work and their lives. I didn't tell anyone what Edgar had said, because I didn't know how to tell something so unusual. I thought old Edgar would never have said anything untrue in his whole life.

CHAPTER 33

On a bus from Norwich, coming home after Saturday fun, with Neville beside me on the window seat, we took quick glimpses at the magazine I'd bought, called *Health and Efficiency*. It was pocket-size, so we could hold it low. Nobody else would see, if we took care. The photographs were black-and-white, with shadows hiding parts we might have wanted most to see. The conductress was looking at tickets or selling them. We were well towards the back. When she was close, quite suddenly, my caution went. She looked to see what it was we'd had our heads down for, said something like, 'What have you got?' I showed, page open, the best one there, good to see, but with deep black shadows, skilfully. I knew who the conductress was. Her younger sister had been at grammar school with me.

'You boys,' she said, or something like that, looked quickly at our tickets, smiling, pleased by what she'd seen, the picture, and two boys surprised. I knew I'd wanted her to see, and she knew too.

With Neville under a willow at the Green end of the Rod Alley pit, I could not know that this was a last time. We were not doing anything in particular because as usual there was not much in particular to do. We were just talking a bit, and Neville said he had a headache.

'My old skull don't half ache.' He said he thought the best thing to do would be to go home.

He went home and I never saw him again. I think it was the next day he died, or the day after that, from meningitis. He had been my best friend, the only one of the early friends who was still there after I was separated from them all somewhat by going to grammar school when I was thirteen. I had always known him.

Mr Oliver caught up with me. I had come out of the churchyard on my own, leaving Neville in the hole in which he had just been put, with all the people standing there dazed with sadness. Mr Oliver was feeling like me, just wanting to be away.

We were on the path by the Ottermer pit, going in the direction of Rod Alley and the White Horse. He said something kindly, knowing my feelings. Then he said:

'You know, John, I never heard that boy Neville say a word against anybody.'

I said no. Mr Oliver was not a man who said much. He was feeling like me, that there was nothing much we could say to each other. He must have been very glad to have given Neville the pleasure of riding his horses. I was feeling guilty that I had told Mrs Petley that Neville sometimes went riding when he should have caught the bus to Norwich for work. What I felt most, was that it was Neville back there in that hole in the ground, not me.

ACKNOWLEDGEMENTS

"PLAY TO ME GYPSY (THE SONG I LOVE)"
Words and Music by JIMMY KENNEDY and KAREL VACEK
© 1932, Reproduced by permission of EMI Music Publishing Limited, London W8 5SW

"ROLL ALONG COVERED WAGON"
Words and Music by JIMMY KENNEDY
© 1934, Reproduced by permission of EMI Music Publishing Limited, London W8 5SW

"RED SAILS IN THE SUNSET" Words and Music by JIMMY KENNEDY and WILHELM GROSZ
©1935, Reproduced by permission of EMI Music Publishing Limited, London W8 5SW and by permission of Peter Maurice Music Co Ltd and Redwood Music Ltd 25% interest in respect of the Estate of William Grosz for the territories of the United Kingdom and all territories within The Commonwealth of Nations (including Canada, Australia, New Zealand and Hong Kong), Eire, South Africa and Spain